AND THIS IS TRUE
EMILY MACKIE
German Boy
HADLEY
OUME ROAD
MILLS
D0205967

GRANTA

12 Addison Avenue, London W11 4QR | email editorial@granta.com
To subscribe go to www.granta.com, or call 845-267-3031 (toll-free 866-438-6150)
in the United States, 020 8955 7011 in the United Kingdom

ISSUE 120: SUMMER 2012

In the United States, *Granta* is published in association with Grove/Atlantic Inc., 841 Broadway, 4th Floor, New York, NY 10003 and distributed by PGW. All editorial queries should be addressed to the London office.

Granta, ISSN 173231, is published four times per year by Granta Publications, 12 Addison Avenue, London W11 4QR.

The 2012 US annual subscription price is $48. Airfreight and mailing in the USA by agent named Air Business Ltd, c/o Worldnet Shipping Inc., 156–15, 146th Avenue, 2nd Floor, Jamaica, NY 11434, USA. Periodicals postage paid at Jamaica, NY 11431.

US POSTMASTER: Send address changes to *Granta*, Air Business Ltd. c/o Worldnet Shipping Inc. 156–15, 146th Avenue, 2nd Floor, Jamaica, NY 11434.

Subscription records are maintained at *Granta* Magazine, c/o Abacus e-Media, PO Box 2068, Bushey, Herts WD23 3ZF.

Air Business is acting as our mailing agent.

Granta is printed and bound in Italy by Legoprint. This magazine is printed on paper that fulfils the criteria for 'Paper for permanent document' according to ISO 9706 and the American Library Standard ANSI/NIZO Z39.48-1992 and has been certified by the Forest Stewardship Council (FSC). *Granta* is indexed in the American Humanities Index.

ISBN 978-1-905881-61-1

CONTENTS

GRAND ROUNDS

Chris Adrian

Thank you, Kate, for that really nice introduction. I don't think anyone but my mom has ever said such kind things about me, and she only says them when she's drunk. I'm kidding! She stopped drinking a couple days ago. I'm sorry I'm late and that I kept you waiting. I know very well you all have a lot of work to do.

But it's really neat to be here, having grown up at UCSF as a resident and now as a fellow. I used to fall asleep in those same seats during lectures just like this one. That is to say, I won't hold it against you, residents, if you fall asleep this morning. Though I find myself becoming curmudgeonly about work-hour revisions and glorifying the good old bad old days of training when we still worked thirty-six hours straight compared to your twelve. OK, twenty . . . but still . . .

I change the title of this talk a lot. Today it's called 'The Teddy Bears' Picnic', but sometimes I call it 'Why Stories Matter', and sometimes I call it 'The Worst Year of My Life', and sometimes 'Theory and Practice at the Intersection of Art and Medicine'. So I'll start by reviewing what people in academic settings say when they talk about stories and medicine and then I'll talk about how and why people I respect and trust insist that a facility in telling and listening to stories makes for a better practice of medicine. After that I want to read you this story I wrote about sick teddy bears and the rebel angels and the hospital staff who have to try to take care of the teddy bears and the angels and themselves after they all get caught in a shrink ray. And then I'll tell you a little bit about the worst year of my life, as it related to that story, and you won't be surprised to hear that that worst year coincided with my first year of a Pediatric Oncology Fellowship. So, that's what's behind the title. More about that later.

My slides are out of order. I'm sorry. I came here right from the airport, hence the lateness. It was a family emergency.

So. What do we do with stories in medicine? Oops . . . out of order again. My mom was sick. That was the family emergency, or I would have had these in order. Here we go. 'Narrative Medicine'. What does that even mean, 'Narrative Medicine'? I'm never totally sure what that means, but I think that's part of the point, that it means different things to different people, and that, just because the phrase 'Narrative Medicine' contains the word 'medicine' you can't expect it to mean the same thing to everyone like some words or phrases do, like 'bezoar' or 'Munchausen's syndrome by proxy'. I think being ambivalent about what it means is OK – this is a little cartoon I found with Cerberus the dog. Believe it or not I had a toy poodle named Cerberus when I was a kid. We had him trained so if you said, 'Cerberus, kill!' he would jump up on someone's lap and lick their face. My mom thought that was hilarious. The slide didn't come out very well but you can see he's sitting on his therapist's couch and the therapist is asking him how he feels. And one head says 'Good!' and one head says 'Bad!' and the middle head says 'Ambivalent!' And then in the next panel they're both just sitting there and in the last one the therapist says, 'It's good to see that you're getting in touch with your feelings.' And I put it in there just to underscore this idea of ambivalence or to show that it's OK to be ambivalent. As if such things were proved by cartoons. But maybe they are. Sorry, that seemed like such a great slide when I was throwing this together. But the point is that this stuff is all very confusing from the time you open your mouth to start talking about it, and that in most ways that's OK – if what people talk about when they talk about Narrative Medicine was easy to say they wouldn't need stories to say it. But in some ways I think that, for me as a writer, trying to explain or understand this is like one of Jane Goodall's chimps trying to give you a lecture on Clifford Geertz. I am more of a practice person than a theory person. Not that there's anything wrong with theory people. I love theory people. My ex is a theory person.

In any case, I think what most of the theory people are saying is just that they want us to listen to our patients, to get some intimation of the shape and scope of their lives, and that stories – writing them, telling them, listening to them – can help us do that. And of course we listen to our patients. But then again, we don't. To borrow a phrase from this guy – sorry, that's not him. Sorry, I am a bit of a mess from this family emergency and am functionally more than a little post-call. This was supposed to be a joke, that I prefer this Paul – McCartney – to this Paul – *there we go* – who was Saul of Tarsus before he was Paul of Rome by way of Damascus, Ephesus, Corinth and elsewhere. To borrow a phrase from him: 'God gave them a spirit of stupor, eyes so that they could not see and ears so that they could not hear, to this very day.' What I mean – what people who talk about this mean – is that the dispiriting ordinary and extraordinary everyday transactions of medicine give us a spirit of stupor, and some conscious discipline is required to shake it off.

Yes, Kate? What? The teddy bears? Oh yes, they're coming. I'm getting a bit short on time already, but I'll read fast. And it's a pretty short story.

So what do you do with this notion that we ought to listen to our patients' stories, when it's hard to actually listen, when there are a whole lot of reasons why it's hard? Well, here is a lady I met at a conference on writing and medicine, in Oregon. I was late to that too, actually also because my mom was sick. I missed Dr DasGupta's talk, but she very kindly let me see her slides. I watched them all alone in the auditorium, very late at night, and thought about them for rather a long time there in the dark. I couldn't sleep anyway.

This is a little chart from an article in *Academic Medicine* that Dr DasGupta wrote. She's talking about what they do at Columbia with this – what they do when they try to teach their students to tell stories and listen to stories. They have a whole department of Narrative Medicine there, which kind of blows my mind every time I think about it. Can you imagine being able to call *that* consult?

But this chart is about a class they run for the second years. A *required* class – where they spend six weeks in a humanities seminar.

You can see from the chart what they're doing with their six weeks. They come to class with some idea for an illness narrative, a story of illness. It can be their own, but it doesn't have to be. In fact, they are encouraged to use someone else's story. My mom was sick for weeks this last time, but I could only get away to see her recently. There's an illness narrative for you.

So you can see that Dr DasGupta has them try different things with the story. She sets up some hoops and asks them to jump through, as it were. Try writing from the point of view of the patient's body or even a body part. Try switching up the genre – write the story as a poem or a regular essay or a TV show or a commercial or a play. We had an interesting discussion about how her students sometimes only discover what they want to tell, how they discover what part of the story really matters, as they switch it or carry it from form to form and find which part stays the same amid all the changes. I told her I was working on something that started as a story and became a novel and then an essay before it was finally a graphic novel about the demon that possesses Linda Blair in *The Exorcist*, but that it was really about my mother. And Dr DasGupta said, 'Exactly!' It's about a lady who keeps having sex with this demon, so her kids are all half demon, and they have to sort of figure that out and deal with that. It's called *Pazuzu* because that was the demon's name. Everyone always thinks it's supposed to be Satan who possesses Linda Blair, but it's Pazuzu. Poor Linda Blair. There's an illness narrative for you, too.

So you can see that in Dr DasGupta's course there's a kind of schedule of mutation and permutation to the story the students are telling. Yes, Kate? What's the difference between mutation and permutation? Never mind. In the last week of the course, the syllabus says, 'Try to reconcile these different versions of the story that you've told.' Which leads, as you might imagine, to a whole discussion about what 'reconcile' means in this context. Kate's about to start a chant, 'Teddy bears! Teddy bears!' They're coming, I swear. One more slide. OK, two more slides.

This is a 'Theory of Empathy'. I'm not totally sure what I think about this. I suppose I included it because I needed a fancy slide. This gentleman is from NYU – Martin Hoffman. I think he's a social psychologist or a developmental psychologist. This is just a short extract from a book called *Empathy and Moral Development.* So he defines empathy as involving a psychological process that makes an individual have feelings which are more congruent with another's situation than his or her own. That's reasonable, I think. But what psychological process?

[THIRTY-SECOND SILENCE]

Sorry. Suddenly this slide doesn't make very much sense to me. I think I already told you I . . . that I'm functionally post-call. But I wonder if it would make sense even if the past few days had not been the past few days. I may just be resistant to theories of empathy. So you see these terms up there. 'Empathic Distress' and 'Mediated Association' and 'Role-Taking' and 'Sympathetic Distress'. And empathic distress is what you get when you see someone suffering and it makes you uncomfortable. The psychological distress, as Mr Hoffman calls it. And mediated association involves feeling that same sort of discomfort even though you're not right in front of the person – you're just hearing their story somehow, or you're listening to 'We Are the World'. Role-taking involves adopting that person's point of view, whether on your own initiative or because someone tells you to do it or makes you do it. And then sympathetic distress is what you get when you're uncomfortable and it's more about them than about you. I think that's what he's saying. The 'motive to comfort oneself', he says, 'is transformed into a desire to help'. So it's a process. Empathic distress becomes sympathetic distress by means of mediated association. I don't know. That all sounds perfectly reasonable, but I guess it leaves me cold. It seems kind of like saying that a Volkswagen pulled up in your driveway and forty-five people got out but neglecting to mention that they were all clowns. Or saying your daughter is ill and neglecting to mention that she is possessed by

Pazuzu. Or saying that your mom died and neglecting to say that she starved herself to death and you let her do it. I mean, I think it's very important to try to approach these nebulous mysterious processes systematically and reductively to understand what's actually going on with them, but something in me always feels a little deflated and unconvinced by the results. Maybe because it seems like you always have to throw out the mysterious part or just ignore it in order to make your reduction or systematization successful. I didn't read the book, though – *Empathy and Moral Development*. I didn't read it. And I should admit to you that, the picture of Mr 'of Tarsus' notwithstanding, I've never read the whole Bible. Which is one of my problems, I guess, that I never read the book, or the whole book. And I'm just sort of winging it, in the ethics and morality department.

We're only about three minutes away from the teddy bears now.

This is the last slide, which talks about the University of Michigan's FCE programme.

[FORTY-FIVE-SECOND SILENCE]

Sorry. I'm sorry again. I'm trying to remember what FCE stands for and for some reason all I can think of is Fancy Cat Entrepreneur. But that's not it. Fostering Clinical Empathy? Family Clinical Education? Something like that. The Michigan folks – they're doing something a little different than Dr DasGupta, pairing their narrative enterprise with a patient encounter. They send their students out to families for a sort of preceptorship. The students visit patients in their homes and ask them questions like, 'What's it like to only have one foot?' You can see the programme there: six visits over two years – not that many, I suppose. Small groups with a clinician facilitator. They're evaluated on the basis of essays and on the feedback from the patients, so it goes in their file if they are good at visiting, or good listeners, or make friends with their patients. And likewise a patient can report, 'This person has got the personality of a hibernating lizard,' and it gets recorded. This stuff is all from an article in *Academic Medicine* from

July of 2008 by one of the architects of the Michigan programme, Dr Kumagai. The last bit is an extract from the discussion section, where authors of the papers support their pedagogical strategy with educational theory. 'The physical presence of, and interactions with, another human being whose life is profoundly affected by chronic illness, as well as the story he or she tells, may foster an interpersonal link in affective, cognitive and experiential domains. This, in turn, will enhance perspective taking, and serve as the basis for a hot cognition for empathic feelings between the learner and another individual.'

Yes, Kate? What's a hot cognition? Well . . .

[FORTY-SECOND SILENCE]

I don't think I remember the exact definition. It sounds very sexy though, doesn't it? But I believe it's about your thought process becoming emotionally charged. And that charge makes the learning stick. I suppose in this context it would go something like, 'Oh my gosh, this patient whose home I'm currently visiting has no feet and that makes me remember the time that my mother broke my ankle with a hammer and how awful that was,' and so the bonds of empathy are formed. It's not that simple, of course. I mean, I'm making it sound like they're oversimplifying the whole process because I don't understand the theory they're deploying, and just because I've lost my faith in such endeavours and ideas doesn't mean they're not useful or good or true. I think what they're saying is . . . I mean, the reason I meant to talk about this in the first place is that they are flinging stories around in this programme because they believe that their students will respond to them in a way that will foster their native empathy. The students will meet these people and hear these stories and have a hot cognition flash and take someone else's role and move from empathic distress to sympathetic distress. What they're describing is beautiful, if you can believe it, that you can learn to care about people by listening to their stories, and that the problem in the world of medicine and the world of the world is not a dearth of caring but a shortage of stories. I like to think about that being true, but I have a hard time with it. I have a hard time believing that stories ever make that kind of difference, and most of the time it's easier to believe that despite appearances nobody ever really hears what anyone else is saying, and that there are no listeners in the world of stories, just a dispiriting over-abundance of tellers, and everybody is ululating in some very private language that sounds to anybody else like alien hiccups. And maybe that is all just another way to say that no one really knows how to listen to these stories.

Which brings us to the teddy bears. Finally! I'm almost out of time, I know. I wanted to read you this whole story, but I'll just do part of it. So there is this one last slide, which is a picture of my mom. There she is. This is from a long time ago, from back when she was a hot cognition, so to speak. She's wearing a flight attendant's uniform because she used to be a flight attendant, before I was born. Except she never liked it when people said flight attendant. She preferred to be called a stewardess. Flight attendants are old and have turkey wattles, she said, but stewardesses are beautiful and forever young. I'm showing this picture of her because this was her story, in a sense. The Teddy Bears' Picnic was this episode from her hot young adulthood that involved two heroin-addled jazz musicians and my Aunt Chris, who wasn't her sister, just a friend from childhood with whom she had young-adult adventures. I don't know exactly what happened on this picnic – she would never tell, but from the hints she gave my sister and me, we constructed a story of roly-poly jazz druggies and a lot of wine and a semen-stained picnic blanket. So that's where this story starts, with my mom. And I won't set it up any more, but I'll talk more in a few minutes about the other ways it came together, how it's about my dead patient and my own life at the time I wrote it. So.

'It was time once again for the Teddy Bears' Picnic.'

[A FULL MINUTE OF SILENCE, THEN TENTATIVE APPLAUSE]

Wait, wait, sorry! Sorry. That's not it. Not the end, I mean. That would be pretty silly, if that were the whole story. It must sound like I don't know what comes next, but I have it right here written out. This is going to sound very strange, but I was trying to decide whether or not I should tell you that my mom died yesterday, and then I was trying to decide if I had already told you. I suppose that's how post-call I am. Anyway, it seemed very important to the story that I tell you that. Like I was being dishonest or disingenuous somehow by not saying that. Did I tell you already? I didn't think so. Is it weird for me to tell you? I guess it is weird, but it felt equally weird not to tell you. I know more than half of you by name, after all, and you know me. It's why I was so late, because she was dying, and then she was dead. And since this story starts with her, it was important for you to know. And now we're almost out of time. I'll start again.

'It was time once again for the Teddy Bears' Picnic.'

[DR KATE MATTHAY RISES FROM HER SEAT AND OFFERS THE SPEAKER A TISSUE]

Thank you, Kate. Sorry. You know, I don't think I should read this story. I'll do another one. As much as I have of it, anyway. I was working on this new story on the plane. You'll probably say, you should have been working on this horrible talk. But I couldn't sleep. I was exhausted, but I couldn't sleep. So I'll just tell you about the teddy bear story. I'll sum it up. It's not that great, anyway. There are these bears and a little girl and some aliens and a shrink ray. And her doctors get shrunk and have an adventure inside her body and there are some magic ponies who are ultimately responsible for all the sickness and confusion and unhappiness in the girl and the hospital and in this country. I guess you have to read it or hear it to really make sense of it, for it not to sound totally ridiculous. But the important part is that there was something about this story that I once thought married my own troubles with the troubles of my patient, this poor doomed six-year-old girl with a brain tumour. I was away in Boston stalking my ex-boyfriend the last time she got sick, and I happened to get back on the night she died. I went from the airport right to her room but she had been dead for hours. I said something to her parents about how I believed they had made the right decisions on her behalf and how much I respected them and admired them, and how much I would miss her, and these were all true statements. And walking home I bawled my head off, but I didn't know if I was crying because this little girl had died or because my ex had told me to stop stalking him, that dogs would marry cats before he consented to get back together with me, that Pat Robertson would have a snowball party in hell before he wanted to get back together, that he wanted me to go away and never come back, so I kept hearing him say that, like Good Gollum says to Evil Gollum in *The Lord of the Rings* when that poor creature is having his psychotic break. Go away and never come back! Go away and never come back!

And while I was walking home I kept asking him to come back, calling his name out loud, except intermittently I was using this little girl's name instead. Even as I said it, over and over, I thought, *How strange*, and *What am I doing?* I got home and made a sort of rehearsal of a suicide. I sat around for a while with a telephone cord around my neck, not tied to anything. Oh, I tied it to the shower rod for a while and I tied it to a pull-up bar for a while but I also tied it to my ankle, and to a teapot and to the cat. I even tied it to my balls, and how was that supposed to put me out of my misery? After that night I sort of had a nervous breakdown for the next few weeks. A relatively functional one, I suppose, though poor Dr Lauchle, who was stuck on service with me, would probably disagree since she was the one doing the work all day while I was crying in the bathroom. But the point of this story is not that I was crazy, which I suppose I am in many ways, or that a Heme/Onc Fellowship makes you want to kill yourself, which I suppose it does in many ways, but that for a few moments there I didn't know who my heart was breaking for. And

I was going to tell you – when I give this talk I usually tell people – that the story, with the teddy bears and the aliens, was somehow about those few moments, that it made some kind of useful sympathetic noise. But now . . . today . . . in this last hour, actually, that seems like the wrong thing to say, and the wrong story to tell.

The other story . . . the new story . . . goes something like this: 'When I was a child I wanted to be sick. This was partly because my mother, who was not always nice to her children, was always nice to me when I was sick. She was often sick herself, though almost never actually unhealthy, the important exception of course being that she had breast cancer while she was carrying me and was treated with a mastectomy just a few weeks before I was delivered. But it was also because sick people – and especially sick children – were special, and I wanted to be special.'

That's all I have. And I'm out of time. I know. Kate is pointing at her watch. I'm almost done. There's no more of that story written down, but I can tell you what happens in it . . . I can sum up the important parts. In this story the narrator's mother breaks his ankle with a hammer and takes him to the emergency room when he's three. It's the first of a bunch of treatments. I mean, that's what she calls them. She says she is making him better, which in some twisted sense she is, since he actually likes being sick. He gets a fever in the hospital, and they think he has osteomyelitis, but it's his mom pooping in his IV or whatever, and this whole thing starts, this whole long thing starts, where she puts him in the hospital again and again.

And then . . . this is where before, in the old story, the evil magic ponies would usually come in, because what kind of child could ever conceive of such an action, or plan it out, or take any satisfaction in it? This kid, who is eight or nine at this point, walks into his mother's bedroom one night and breaks *her* ankle with a baseball bat. And she shrieks and writhes in her bed – how she cried and cried with her pillow clutched over her face! It was like she was smothering herself. But when she can talk she says to the kid, 'Go call the ambulance. Mommy's fallen down the stairs.'

So it goes on that way, years and years more of it, though there's a father intermittently in the house and a sister. They're not oblivious, but they're powerless, like they always are – we've met these people in our practice, we know this, we forgive them for being powerless as a matter of course. It escalates and wanes and escalates and maybe it gets stranger. Like, when he's thirteen she makes him a strawberry shortcake, though he's developed a horrible strawberry allergy, with full-blown anaphylaxis, and he sits down quietly in the kitchen and forks it up. And he has gotten in the habit of making her morning tea when his father is away, and one day he cuts it half and half with silver cleaner, and she sips it nonchalantly, reading the paper in bed while he stands in her door, watching. Years and years this goes on! His chart is 859 pages long. Hers is over 1,000.

And then it stops. I can't even remember when exactly, and he doesn't even remember why. At some point, much later, he'll think it's like falling out of love with someone, when you look at them and think, 'Why did I ever go out with that person?' and you think of what you did with them and ask yourself, 'Why did I ever do that?' It's like that. Why did I ever do that? Probably she's saying the same thing. Why did I ever do that to my child? Years pass again. Years and years and years, and I suppose they have a relatively normal relationship. OK, not really, but it's civil, and no one goes to the hospital until after his father dies, and his mother gets sick all by herself. She stops eating, more or less, and he goes home a few times to try to turn things around, and yes there is silver cleaner under the kitchen sink still but that is neither here nor there. It doesn't mean anything. He looks at it but doesn't really even see it. He tries to make her better. He, a paediatrician now, has adventures in adult medicine. She goes home from the hospital. Years pass again. Not many, though. Barely two, when she's back in the hospital.

Now she's very ill. She might not have gotten quite so ill if someone had come to help her again. He was very busy in his first year of Oncology Fellowship, and having a nervous breakdown et cetera, et cetera. His sister couldn't go help, though it really was her turn, because she has a terrible aversion to their mother. In the past few years she's conveniently manifested a paralysing compulsion to avoid anything to do with the lady. She can't even get letters from her any more – they are filthy. They are contaminated. She'd have to be wearing a moonsuit to handle a letter from her mother. She can't even touch the *postman* any more. In fact, she can't even tolerate the idea of their mother any more, so it's very hard to talk about her when he calls to say, she's quite sick. His sister tells him that's a terrible tragedy. And then she tells him how she can't even be near sexy stewardesses, or witty mean old ladies who smoke a lot. Even her name – Margaret – is hard to tolerate. She has so many friends named Margaret, and they're all wondering what they've done to drive her away, but they haven't done anything.

He goes back to Florida – horrible old Florida. Has anything good ever come out of Florida? He probably landed just as she was being transferred to the ICU, and when he arrives in the hospital she is already having blood-pressure issues. They had allowed her to refuse antibiotics and most diagnostic interventions, though she was clearly septic, and though she was depressed out of her mind, but once she was no longer responsive they got it all started up, so she's on triple antibiotics when he arrives and there has been a nice little workup, and they are just starting inotropes. He thinks that is a little odd, that they let her refuse all those things, but what does he know? He is a paediatrician, used to overpowering toddlers so he can look in their throats for diphtheria. He arrives in the ICU and the doctor says to him, Welcome, welcome, next of kin! What shall we do?

He gets into bed with his mom, and thinks of his sister. This would be terrifically horrible for her, to hold their mother when she's barely clothed, and smelly in that funny way that people get smelly in the ICU, when you can appreciate the careful and attentive washing of the body that the clinical assistants perform, but then under that, sometimes subtle and sometimes strong, is a horrible rotten stench. She looks awful too, like she's already dead, like she ought to be cold as a corpse, though in fact she is putting off a terrible heat. She looks just like the

Crypt Keeper, if you remember him, the host of *Tales from the Crypt*, and he very much expects her to sit up and say, in that characteristic cackling shriek, 'Welcome, kiddies! Would you like to dance to the death?' But she doesn't say anything of the sort. She opens her eyes and looks at him but does not seem to see him, and when he says, 'I love you, Mom. What do you want?' and 'I love you, Mom. What should I do?' she doesn't reply, except he thinks it's possible that she sneers at him a little, as if to say, Why are you bothering to ask? You know what I want. The same thing that you do. You've always known.

So he gets out of the bed and tells the doctor, I'm ready now. And they call in the team which includes the respiratory therapist and a nurse and a chaplain and some lady with black hair swept back from her face like the wings of a raven, and huge, dark soul-sucking eyes, dressed like a nineteenth-century Jesuit missionary to Canada, who may be a figment of his imagination or may be a representative from the palliative care team. And even beyond the curtain and the room it's like he can feel the whole hospital and hear them singing 'Kill her! Kill her!' as sweetly as the Whos in Whoville ever sang 'Fah who foraze! Dah who doraze! / Welcome Christmas, Christmas Day!' And he is thinking that this is a perfect ending, and a perfect story, that they both should get what they want, and that everyone should approve, and then everyone should be so very happy about it. 'Shall I write the order?' he asks the doctor, and the doctor says, 'I have already done it.'

As a child, after he had been hospitalized a few times, he started to state his 'chief complain' in the emergency room. The triage nurse would say, 'And what's bothering you today?' and he would say, 'My chief complain is osteomyelitis' or 'My chief complain is a small bowel obstruction' or 'My chief complain is intractable pain' or even, when he was a snarky teenager, 'You are bothering me. You are my chief complaint.' And the nurse would smile or grimace or frown but always, whoever she was, unless he had insulted her, she would say something like, 'Oh my, you're going to be a doctor one day, aren't you?' And he would say, 'Of course.'

After his mother is dead. After he has written back to his sister, who kept texting him over and over, 'Is she dead yet? Is she dead yet?' After the terrible heat has left his mother's body, he gets out of her bed and, ignoring the condolences and questions of the nurse, he leaves the ICU bay and the ICU and leaves the hospital to walk in the merciless Florida sunshine in a short loop through the parking lot to the Emergency Room entrance. He sits until they call him out of his chair and the triage nurse sizes him up with a sweeping glance and says, 'What's the matter, honey?' He stares at his feet and she asks again, but he doesn't answer. 'What can we help you with?' she tries and 'What brings you in today?' but he's still silent. She gets slightly frustrated, though never stops calling him honey. It's like she senses that it is hard to say, or hard to know. It's her, he thinks suddenly. She is the good thing that is finally going to come out of Florida. She asks again, What's wrong? What is it? How can we help you? What's your complaint? And finally, when the other nurses have begun to watch curiously and the security guard has come hovering closer and closer, he looks up and says to her perm, 'I don't know.'

So that's a better story. That's better than magic ponies and teddy-bear picnics and whatever else that other one was about – I can't even remember any more because this one is better. This one is *perfect*. Do you understand why it's perfect? Not because it's true. You can never know if it's true or not. It's because the story and the life that it's based upon are the same thing. Because the story and the troubling thing that gave birth to it are the same thing. Because the story and the trouble are the same thing.

Does this make any sense at all? Kate is shaking her head no. Thank you for staying, Kate. Thank you, everybody. I know you have places to be. I know that the people who left have places to be. I'm grateful that nobody's called a chaplain code on me and that the psychiatrists in the audience have remained seated with their Thorazine injectors safely contained even though you probably all think I'm having a nervous breakdown up here, which maybe I am. I keep saying I'm functionally post-call but I guess it feels more like I'm post-everything, like there's this state of post-ness that the extreme difficulty of the past few days has allowed me to enter, and it's not about fatigue or being fed up with things but more about the advent of a kind of clarity. Maybe a hallucinatory clarity, but probably a transient clarity. All the way back here on the plane I kept thinking, this is the story. This is the story to tell them. Because it is perfect and because those other stories – everything I've written, everything I've seen written, though keep in mind I never finish books and I quote from the Bible without having read it – are the wrong stories to tell because they are not perfect. But what do you do with that perfect story, that starts the first time your mother breaks your bones and ends when you kill her? Do you empathize with it? Can you empathize with it? Do you sit down with the whirlwind and say, 'That must be very difficult for you. That whirling. It must make you feel ungrounded. I empathize with your terrible, terrible whirliness'? Or do you cower? Or run away? Or say nothing but silence?

What do you say? I wish somebody . . . I wish one of you would tell me. Kate? Rob? Mignon? Clay? Anu? You in the back, with the Coco Chanel hair. I don't know your name but I know your face and I will never forget your hairdo. I've seen you moping around the ICU all year and never learned your name, but every day I thought to myself, 'That lady is the very avatar of sympathy,' because every time you come out of a room you look like it's *your* mother in the bed. Will you tell me? No? Then you, behind her, with the bolo tie. I don't recognize you at all. Are you an oncologist? Are you even a paediatrician? You don't have to be, don't worry. And of course sometimes it's the mysterious stranger who shows you the answer you're looking for, cupped like a spider between his two hands. Will you tell me what to say? Open your hands? Not you either? O Stranger! O Patient! O Self! Won't one of you tell me what to say? Won't anybody? Please, tell me?

[TWO MINUTES OF SILENCE. THE SPEAKER IS LED AWAY FROM THE PODIUM BY DR MATTHAY.] ■

Dilation

I

We need to harness the vaguely erotic disappointment that attends
the realization you aren't being followed,
keys gripped between the fingers, ready to strike at the eyes
The after-image of byzantine gold leaf dissolving in the trees when
we emerge from the museum must be harnessed,
and the delicate carnation of the sky at the rooftop screening,
and the dress of the hostess, its exploration of formative drives

If you are anything like me, you emerge from the hospital's automatic
doors into the heat and glare of its parking lot
unable to recall the colour of the rental or the demands of practical
reason
You surface from the subway to find it's fully night and hard to
remember the preceding generation's claims
for disjunction, you saw the child of a Turkish diplomat fall from a
penthouse balcony,
curled up on a floor model at the SoHo Crate & Barrel when you
received the terrible news

from a poem that probably dates from 1939, address to an adjacent
posterity
Green eyeshadow and surprising gentleness of the saleswoman who
asks if I'm OK must be harnessed if we
are to surpass camp and apathy, plain-clothes security closing in
You feel emancipated briefly from fragmentation when the D train
emerges onto the Manhattan Bridge,
vertically polarized light entering the water, seventy-six storeys of
rippled steel refusing to be actual

all at once, stand and offer your seat to an old man who isn't there,
    listen politely to his demand for a theatre
that combines distance and empathy, false proscenium lit to reveal
evaporating value, the delicate carnation that follows heat and glare

II

I came into the cities at a time in which the service industry employed
    a swift underclass of Spanish-speaking labourers
I came into the cities when the art world's post-medium pluralism
    valorized stupidity
In the midst of weather patterns of increasing extremity, I came into
    the cities, unsure if I should say *gracias* to the man
refilling my glass, notes of chlorine, antidepressants in trace amounts
One way was enumerating the bad forms of alienated collective
    power: breathing hot particles from Japan,

bundled debt, another way was passing beyond the reach of friends,
    to internalize an allegory,
tracking the dilation where aorta meets heart, minor tremor in the hand
Part of me wants to say there is a mock-oratorical mode capable of
    vitalizing critical agency and part of me
wants to praise the maple's winged samaras, the distance achieved
    from the parent tree,
but mainly I want to argue they're one thing, real if indefensible

like cities in time, spinning as they fall
My role in the slaughter doesn't disqualify the beauty I find in all
forms of sheltered flame, little votive polis,
that I eat while others starve does not refute the promise of dimming
house lights, weird fullness of the instant
before music, that I ventriloquize when I address you *is* the marker of
my voice, important source
of syrup and tonewood, coming to you live

from the ellipses of compotier and vase, grave air of a masterpiece, its
notes of ozone and exhaust,
jasmine in trace amounts, tracking the dilation of new forms
of private temporality into public architecture, glass curtains as they
dim

III

The ideal is visible through its antithesis like small regions of warm
blue underpainting and this is its late
July realization, I'm sorry, I know you were expecting more
I'm not going to lecture the neighbour kid with the hydrant key about
conserving water for posterity
until I can think of a better idea for the spontaneous formation of
a public, however brief
By the time you read this, if you are close enough to read this, if you
are reading this

a threat to the first person was called in, prompting its evacuation,
a panic you should take advantage of
in order to compose a face, test predicates against, walk to Sunset
Park and watch the soft-winged kites
at magic hour when light appears immanent to the lit, warm blue
scattering
in the gaps between buildings and print, you can feel the content
streaming
The ideal is a kind of longitudinal subject in which the poem is a note
saying where I left you keys

and a bottle of green wine, sea-rise visible in the compound eye,
mosaic image, flicker effect
in which objects must move in order to persist, thus the preference of
bees for windblown flowers,
thus the analogy collapses like a colony, prompting its evacuation,
but the formal capacity for likening still shines
through its antithesis, feel it misfiring, vaguely erotic disappointment
that combines
distance and empathy, carnation fading from the contrails, trying
to conceive

in a ready-to-assemble bed as the metropole shifts East
I believe there is a form of apology both corporate and incantatory
that could convene the future it begs for leniency,
inherited dream you can put anything in: antithetical blue, predicate
green

HARDY ANIMAL

M.J. Hyland

A few weeks after I was diagnosed with multiple sclerosis, I made a pact with dying. I wrote draft suicide notes and planned my 'exit'; not because I'd lost a chunk of my physical usefulness – most days, I can't walk more than 200 metres and can't use my right hand for more than a few hours – but because it turns out I'm the worst kind of candidate for an illness like MS.

I thought I was invincible. I'd never needed anybody's help, hadn't needed somebody to carry my suitcase down the stairs, or take out the bins. I didn't bind well to the idea of dependency, to walking sticks and stairlifts. So I made plans: when it looked like a wheelchair might be wanted, I'd pay my debts, write a will and some letters, find a home for my cat, take what was left of my cash and book into the Ritz in New York for a couple of weeks.

I'd have a nice time and live out the kind of fantasy I'd had when I was a kid living in Ballymun, Dublin's pissy, high-rise council estate. I'd fly first class, wear a chic suit, the masculine kind, pinstriped, with tall black boots (if I could walk at all). I'd eat fancy food and smoke in the hotel room, find a casino and play a few high-stakes poker tournaments, take a helicopter ride over the Hudson, rent an MGB convertible and then, when all the fun was done, I'd get into the king-size bed and do what's needed with an 'Exit Bag' (a plastic bag with a drawstring filled with an inert gas, such as helium or nitrogen).

That was 2008, nearly four years ago, and I've mostly got used to my cut-in-half life. But sometimes I still wake – when it's neither dark nor day – my chest covered in sweat, and words like these beating at the walls of me: 'I'm on the way out. I don't want to be on the way out,' and, in the trap and trip of the weak hours, it's as though my body knows more than I do. On 4 June 2008, the day a neurologist told me I have MS, I wasn't at all sure what he meant. I'd seen some public service announcements on Australian TV which featured people in wheelchairs; people with spitty speech impairments, water-clogged mouths, curled hands with sharp, pointed bones. So, I knew that MS could cut your legs off, put you in a wheelchair, but not much else.

The neurologist showed me the MRI scan and the lesions in my brain; the scars, the permanent neuronal damage which means I've got spasticity and weakness in my right foot, and my right hand (my writing hand).

'On average,' the neurologist said, 'it's at least ten to fifteen years before you need a wheelchair.'

Signs of Trouble

In June 2007 I moved from Rome to Manchester with three suitcases stuffed with books. My first semester at the University of Manchester began in September. I walked to a cafe in the mornings, wrote for five or six hours until late afternoon, and took rock-climbing lessons with one of my MA students. There was nothing wrong with my body.

In December, I went to Paris for Christmas and when I left my hotel room to walk along the Seine, my right leg stopped working. After ten minutes or so my leg turned to wood and stayed that way for about half an hour. The next day the same thing happened, and the day after that and, on the third day, I caught a taxi back to the hotel. I couldn't walk more than a mile.

I went back to Manchester, back to my half-furnished terraced house, and my kittenish black cat. The weird weakness wasn't going away, but for about two weeks I ignored it. I could live without walking, I'd make adjustments, and I was sure the problem was temporary.

I started using taxis. I caught them everywhere, and soon the taxi drivers in Chorlton got to know me. When I booked taxis to go on short journeys, I told the driver I'd had a rock-climbing accident, and couldn't walk, not even two blocks. I took taxis to the library, a £3 fare, and gave the driver £6. I called taxis to take me round the corner to the newsagent's to get milk, a £1.90 fare, and gave the driver £5.

'Is your leg not better yet?' asked one of the drivers.

'I need an operation. I might have to wait a while.'

I felt ashamed about the short fares (my father was once a taxi driver), so I rang the local cab company's head office, and told the girl I needed regular taxis for short distances. I told her about my rock-climbing injury and, as I told the lie, I imagined the accident vividly. I was at an indoor rock-climbing centre, and I'd fallen and landed on the blue rubber mats, my right leg twisted beneath me.

'I'll pay tips,' I said.

'You're all right, love,' she said. 'Don't worry about that.'

Then, in January, while I was working on my third novel, my right hand seized up. It quit. After an hour of typing it stiffened and curled, fell limp. Strangest of all, I couldn't use a pen, especially not a ballpoint, for more than a minute or so.

I went to see my GP.

'There's something wrong with my right leg,' I said. 'It turns to wood when I've been walking for about ten minutes.'

He wondered if I was tired.

'I'm never tired.'

I also told him about my hand and he wondered if I might be overdoing it. He told me to report back if the problems persisted.

At the next appointment it was my GP's birthday. There were balloons in his office and he was in a good mood. He told me about his volunteer work with the ambulance service and I liked him all the more for that and found the nerve to tell him about my bladder.

'Sometimes I need to duck down alleyways or go into underground car parks,' I said. 'And I have a few weird problems with my bowels.'

He called for a nurse to act as a chaperone and together they assembled the white screen and the gurney. My GP said to put my knees up under the sheet.

When the nurse left, my GP said me he'd found nothing wrong. He seemed annoyed; not as though he thought I was a Munchausen's case, or a hypochondriac, but just plain annoyed. He turned his swivel chair away from me.

'Something weird's going on,' I said. 'As well as my leg and those urgency problems, I have a burning pain in my right arm.'

He wondered if this might be RSI or tendinitis.

'But would that explain why I'm always dropping things? And what about the strange constriction in my throat, especially when I'm angry or nervous? Like now.'

MS is difficult to diagnose. There's a long list of symptoms and so many of them – fatigue, weakness, dizzy spells, blurred vision, nausea – look and sound like the ordinary things that sometimes strike healthy people. And in many MS patients the symptoms manifest in peculiar and unpredictable ways. But something about the pattern of my symptoms caused my GP to stop tapping his keyboard and book an MRI scan.

A few weeks after the scan I got a letter from the neurology department at Withington Hospital and it said, 'The MRI has revealed significant brain inflammation.'

On 4 June, I waited in the corridor outside a neurologist's office. A pretty girl in her early twenties sat next to me, with her turkey-necked mother opposite. The girl used a walking stick to take the short journey to the bathroom and I watched her with a semi-blind neutrality, no contempt, or pity; no special regard.

In two days, on 6 June, I'd be forty. My head was sore with two things: a vain dread of getting older and the work I needed to do to cure the problems in my third novel. I wasn't worried about seeing the neurologist. Not one bit. Whatever this inflammation was, medicine would wipe it out. I was glad to know the symptoms weren't phantoms. They were glitches and they'd be cured.

The neurologist called me into his office. He was short, about fifty-five, olive-skinned. He might have been Jewish and that made me happy. He looked like the father of one of the smartest Jewish boys

I'd gone out with when I was studying law.

'Take a seat,' he said.

He was polite, and he knew my name, but he didn't have much time. He made this clear by not wasting any. He turned his monitor to face me and I saw the MRI's black-and-white copy of my brain.

'These are the scars of multiple sclerosis,' he said.

He used his pen to point at the blotches in my brain and he looked in my general direction, but he didn't go near my eyes.

'You have multiple sclerosis,' he said.

'Really?'

'You're lucky,' he said. 'Most people are diagnosed in their early twenties.'

What the Hell is Multiple Sclerosis?

MS is an incurable and often progressive disease of the central nervous system (CNS). The CNS controls movement, emotion, sweating, the secretory glands, emptying the bladder and all the vital functions that depend on nerve cells (neurons). The white blotches on my brain are the scars representing permanent damage to my CNS. In short and crude terms, every neuron consists of a cell body and a series of processes including the nerve fibre (axon). Nervous impulses must travel along the axon to link with other neurons and the axons are surrounded by a sheath: a complex chemical called myelin, which is vital to the process of accelerating the conduction along the axon. In MS the myelin is damaged and its damage means that the electrical signals are slowed, retarded, impaired, cut off or blocked altogether.

In an effort to explain MS to lay people, the myelin sheath is often likened to 'the insulation around an electrical wire'. I say MS is like a radio in a black cab which seems never to get a clear signal on the BBC World Service. When the driver switches to the BBC, the sound is scratchy and sometimes drops out altogether, especially when you pass under a bridge or there's an aeroplane overhead. The driver says,

'Sorry, love. The BBC don't work on here,' and so you're stuck with a live broadcast of a Man City v. Liverpool match and you want to cut your head off.

When the neurologist who diagnosed me sensed that I wasn't ready to leave his office, he turned the computer screen away from me.

'Multiple sclerosis,' I said. 'Shit.'

'It might not be as bad as it sounds.'

He told me that there's a broad spectrum of MS, from mild to serious, but it was hard to say what might happen in my case. It was too early to tell whether – in five years, ten years – I wouldn't be able to speak or swallow. But not to worry.

'I'm going to book you in for steroid treatment.'

'OK,' I said.

Joan Didion and Dignitas

When I got home I googled 'famous writers with multiple sclerosis' and Joan Didion was the only recognizable name on the list. I was annoyed that she has relapsing-remitting MS, with symptoms that come and go, and hurt her, but don't ruin her. Jonathan Katz, the creator of the Emmy Award-winning masterpiece, *Dr. Katz*, was on the list too, and he has the worst kind of MS. He can't write much, can't walk much and needs a wheelchair when he appears onstage. I wrote to Jonathan that night and so began our friendship.

Two days later, the day of my birthday, I was in Dublin as a guest of the Dublin Writers' Festival. After my reading to a small audience (about a hundred people) and after signing copies of my novel *Carry Me Down* (four copies), I went back to the hotel to watch TV and choked on some chocolate. I couldn't swallow, my throat had closed and I was sure this meant brainstem damage. I'd end up like Jacqueline du Pré: alone in a wheelchair parked by a drizzling window, silenced, then dead.

I googled 'Dignitas', 'plastic bags' and 'Exit' and, while I was at it, the phone rang. I cleared my throat and did a radio interview (I can't remember who with, or what for) and after I'd finished putting on a good act, all tough-talking, I went back to googling 'brainstem damage' and 'home-made suicide kits'.

My reaction to having MS isn't typical. In that first year, in 2008, and for most of 2009, I was sure that being sick wrecked the careful brick-by-slow-brick version of myself that I'd spent thirty years building; a carefully controlled, hyper-modified being; a sometimes dissociative selfhood made in opposition to my family.

I told very few people about the diagnosis and none – except my GP – knew how dark, how close to death, my mood had become. MS had ruined the good story: the clever, slum survivor narrative. In this story, I'd made myself, dragged my life from nothing into a pretty good something. I was bionic, a physical and psychological mutant; preternaturally strong, tougher and smarter than the faulty dictates and predictors of my shabby genes. The idea of being impaired meant that after all I had done to escape the life I'd been born to, I'd ended up a failure like them, like my family.

My father is illiterate. He's also a drunk, a gambler and a thief. The best part of him is his wit, but that hardly got a chance, and it's all gone now, along with his mind and memory. He's sixty-five and living in the care of the Wesley Mission and he has Korsakoff's syndrome, a neurological disease caused by alcohol abuse and malnutrition. He's five foot nothing and wears thick lenses. His green eyes seem distorted and enlarged, and as he gets older and loses more and more weight, his eyes get eerier, like the eyes of a terrible deep-sea fish. I haven't seen or spoken to him for more than ten years.

My brother is also illiterate and even more bent out of shape than my father; a violent criminal, a drunk and a part-time junkie. Like my father, he's spent most of his life in prisons, psychiatric hospitals or living rough. I haven't seen or spoken to him for more than fifteen years.

My mother grew up in Dublin polio hospitals – ten years in cots – trained for nothing by Catholic nuns. From the age of five – the day she fell into a pond in Wexford and 'caught' polio – to the age of fifteen, she hardly moved at all. For some of that time she was in an iron lung and was twice given extreme unction. She walks with a sideways limp, and can't stand with her feet flat to the floor because when she was a child her ankles were hobbled by a surgeon. This ankle-breaking procedure, normal in the 1940s, was designed to allow girls struck down with polio to wear high heels when they 'grew up'.

She lives in a weatherboard bungalow now, with my forklift-driving stepfather, and in their nervous, small lives, they have nothing to spare. They fret and scrimp and scrounge. Their best furniture is covered with beach towels and they've little to read but Al-Anon pamphlets and cowboy westerns. When something goes wrong, there's a platitude to salve the pain and stop the thinking: 'Count your blessings' or 'Live and let live'. In her schema, there's God, of course, who works in such mysterious ways that sons turn into criminal madmen even though nobody did anything wrong.

My mother made a slave of herself to raise me and my brother. She worked every day of her life, in typing pools and sitting on reception desks, and all along she said the same thing: 'All I ever wanted was a happy family.'

I feel profoundly sad for her, for my brother and father, too. But I can't be near them, can't belong to them. I worry for them, dream about them, but I can't talk to them. They frighten me. And so, against this background, having MS felt tantamount to losing, and felt too close to being like them; a failure and a victim. For these reasons, and others, my response to the diagnosis was catastrophic; violently deformed and distorted. I told very few people; I kept it a secret. I didn't want my students to know, or the people who don't like me to say, 'Serves her right,' and I didn't want reviewers of my third novel to write, 'M.J. Hyland, that poor novelist with MS, has done a decent job – all things considered.'

Until now, I haven't written about MS, unless you count suicide notes such as 'From is to was' and the letter that I would send to somebody with keys to my house. (The draft of this letter said, 'I'm very sorry for this, but you'll need to let yourself in. I'll be asleep upstairs.') I also wrote a will and thought about who'd be given the job of finding me. (I ultimately decided I'd leave this job to the police or my GP. I'd ask them to take me off somewhere cold and to make sure my organs were donated.)

I'm ready to talk and write about it now. I'm out of the pit.

Steroids v. Homeopathy

A few weeks after the Dublin Writers' Festival, I was in hospital with a cannula stuck in my hand, getting an IV infusion of high-potency steroids. The five-day infusion of steroids acted as a short-term mood enhancer, reduced brain inflammation and lessened the worst of my symptoms, which were (still are) a hand that freezes after about two hours of writing and a leg that needs to be dragged home after a few hundred metres.

One of the patients in the MS ward was a 24-year-old man with nice muscles (he wore shorts and T-shirts). He was an inpatient, like me. Down the end of the ward, near the Acute Brain Unit, where the TV was, he told me he'd run the London Marathon the year before.

'One morning, I just woke up paralysed,' he said. 'My girlfriend had to rush me to hospital. I couldn't walk for weeks.' The only warning was 'a few months earlier my left eye had gone fuzzy and I couldn't see'.

He'd described two of the most common symptoms of MS: paralysis – usually temporary, yet terrifying – and optic neuritis, partial blindness, usually temporary, but also terrifying. And while I was in hospital, I saw that what the neurologist had told me was true: most people are diagnosed with MS in their twenties and, unlike me, most don't smoke, or despise vegetables, or have sick families. MS takes on the young and the healthy, the fat and the spongy, the tall and short; truck drivers, surgeons, dancers and teachers; people who are no sharper than a muffin, and people who are super smart. It takes on chess players, rugby players, law students, van drivers, doctors, guitarists and people who believe in God.

The only irrefutable fact is that you're much more likely to suffer from MS if you live in the northern hemisphere, more likely still if you live in the north of England, in Scotland or Nova Scotia, and if you've experienced a lack of vitamin D in early childhood. (I spent my childhood in Dublin: no oily fish at teatime and not much sun.) MS is not my punishment for being a smoker, for disowning my family, for being a jerk, or for being an atheist.

In late 2008 I went to a series of information sessions for the 'young and newly diagnosed', a once-a-week-for-six-weeks programme, called something like 'Coping with MS'. The venue was a conference room with purple curtains and red carpet; a chain hotel at the butt-end of Manchester, opposite McDonald's and a casino.

On the fifth night there was a special 'guest speaker', a man with MS. He was about forty, had a pot belly and was wheeled into the room by his skinny girlfriend. During his talk about 'coping with MS' he rubbed his tattooed arm and sobbed. When he'd finished crying and saying things like 'At the end of the day, life goes on', and 'To be honest, you just gotta get on with things', his girlfriend wheeled him out, and they both had a roll-up.

When I got home, I did more googling for 'guaranteed painless suicide methods, preferably with no vomiting'. I found the Hemlock Society and read some forum discussions about 'Exit Bags' and I made notes for future reference.

I went back the next week for the final 'Coping with MS' session. A neurologist had come to chat about new drug treatments. One of the people sitting in the plastic chairs round the conference table, using a free plastic pen and eating free biscuits, was a beautiful, very tall young girl who had told us – when we all introduced ourselves – that her impairment was mild; a tingling in her feet and hands, bouts of numbness and weird dizziness and fatigue that sometimes knocked her out.

After the neurologist talked about self-injecting subcutaneous interferon beta-1a (Rebif) and other drugs, the tall girl offered to drive me home. She told me she was working as a model and had been flying from Milan to Manchester after a 'huge fashion shoot' when she'd realized something was wrong with her body.

'It was weird. I started choking on one of those hard-boiled sugar-free sweets. I just couldn't swallow properly.'

When we got stuck in Trafford football traffic, she told me that she'd been using homeopathy to help with her symptoms.

'I don't buy it,' I said.

'You should,' she said. 'Alternative medicines are much more holistic and, like, sensitive.'

This tall, beautiful girl lives round the corner from me and the last time I saw her – about a year ago – she was using a walking stick. She can't work any more. She has primary progressive MS, the worst kind, and collects a disability pension. She's twenty-three.

The man with the nice muscles I met in hospital when I was getting dosed with steroids has the least disabling form of the disease, known as relapsing-remitting – just like Joan Didion's brand of MS – and he's running marathons again.

2009 and a Brand New Drug

In early 2009 I started using voice-recognition software to write. I put on headphones and used JFK's inaugural speech to train the software to recognize my voice. On the first day, when I was sick of the mess of it, I said: *This is a fucking pile of shit* and the software typed: 'This is a flocking to the pilot sheets.'

After a day of training, recognition reached 99 per cent, but by the end of the month, I knew I wouldn't be able to dictate fiction. Writing fiction is the physical act of pushing words round the page until they lock good and tight. Using speech to write was like doing a jigsaw with mittens on. Turns out I need to use my hand to write fiction. I find the words, feel them out; need pen and paper and the act of typing to put the right words in the right order.

One morning, in early 2009, I got two texts from friends who urged me to listen to the morning news: a new drug was being trialled; perhaps it might even be a cure for MS. The drug was Alemtuzumab, an aggressive immunosuppressant, and though not a cure – it can't reverse neuronal damage – it's the first treatment that promises to halt the progression of the disease.

I sent an email to my neurologist right away and asked him if I could join the drug trial. He was reluctant. The trial was closing soon, and the few places left would be reserved for people with the mildest form of the disease. I called a specialist MS nurse and she was no help at all. She didn't know what I was talking about, couldn't pronounce the name of the drug and didn't know anything about the drug trials.

I went online and found the names of the neurologists and immunologists who'd created the drug. I wrote directly to Dr Alasdair Coles at Cambridge University and he replied with enormous generosity and gave me the names of two neurologists, both of whom were heading up Alemtuzumab trials in their respective hospitals. I wrote to both.

There was a catch. To get on the drug trial I'd need the neurologist who had diagnosed me to write a letter advocating my involvement. He didn't refuse, but remained reluctant. Perhaps he didn't want to give me false hope. And so, I used the worst and best of my pushy, stubborn character, and I got the letter.

About a month later, I was in London meeting the remarkable Professor Gavin Giovannoni, who heads the London trial for Alemtuzumab. After a day of tests, both cognitive and physical, and a new MRI scan, Professor Giovannoni authorized my place on the four-year drug trial.

As with all drug trials, this one is randomized and controlled, and uses two treatment groups selected at random. One group gets the wonder drug, Alemtuzumab, the other gets subcutaneous interferon beta-1a (Rebif), a weaker treatment than Alemtuzumab – but a viable treatment nevertheless.

I can't say which of the two drugs I'm taking. I'm still a patient on the trial (we're in year four, phase four, the final phase, known as the safety phase). Every three months I go to London to get treated and tested. And, every month, a phlebotomy bus comes to my house and a nurse takes blood, my pulse, my blood pressure and a sample of midstream urine. While she waits, my blood gets spun (to separate the plasma) and then a courier collects the samples to send to Genzyme, the company that manufactures the drug. I am also seen regularly by a 'blinded' doctor in London (a doctor who's not permitted to know which of the two drugs I'm using, or have used).

Four times a year – at the Research Clinic at the Royal London and Barts – I'm taken through a battery of tests to measure impairment and disease progression. I take a balance test, a paced auditory selective arithmetic test, walk on a treadmill, take eyesight tests, tests for spasticity and briskness – a sharp implement is dragged along the soles of both feet – and coordination tests. I am no more impaired now than I was when the trial began in 2009, and for an MS sufferer, this is an astonishing and unlikely piece of good news.

The Secret

Until now, I've told only a few people I have MS. Most of my colleagues at the University of Manchester think I drive everywhere and never turn up to departmental meetings, or after-work drinks, or Christmas parties, because I'm lazy, pig-headed, selfish and antisocial. Keeping MS a secret has been pretty easy – so far. When people see me at all, it's because I'm sitting in front of a room full of students, walking the 125 metres between a disabled car park and my office, or the twenty-eight metres from my office to the lecture room, or from the road outside my hotel where the taxi has dropped me off, or getting into the lift to go up to my hotel room even if it's on the first floor, or on the short walk between festival-event tents, or from the taxi into the BBC studio or, on good days, as I walk from my house to the corner shop. For emergencies I tell people I have an ingrown toenail or that I recently had a fall rock climbing (another one). I don't look disabled – not yet.

I don't have some of the usual symptoms of MS such as Lhermitte's sign, the sting of an electrical shock when the head is lowered. I don't have the sensation of 'water pouring down the back of my leg' or, as Jonathan Katz also once told me: 'the feeling you get when you park the car and step out and you think you're still moving, and so is the car, everything is spinning and moving'. And although my right leg still turns to wood, becomes weak and inert after a few minutes of walking (often after less than a block), I don't have drop foot and I don't fall over.

And I don't have debilitating fatigue – not any more. In 2011, I discovered Modafinil (Modalert/Provigil), a neuro-enhancer used to treat narcolepsy and sleep apnoea. I take 400mg of this drug every day, and it means I can write longer and don't need to sleep so much. Modafinil works, and Professor Giovannoni is happy for me to use it. But, in the UK, Modafinil is an off-licence drug, and my GP can't (and won't) prescribe it. So, like many with MS and Parkinson's who've discovered the efficacy of Modafinil, I've no choice but to order the drug online and take the risk of being fed duds, sugar pills or worse.

The MS symptom that hurts me the most is Uhthoff's syndrome: it makes me heat-intolerant and means I can't take hot baths or showers – not ever – and in warm weather, I'm fucked.

In August 2011, I was a guest of the Byron Bay Writers' Festival and so was Tim Ferguson, the Australian comedian and TV presenter who 'came out' a few years ago with the news that he has MS.

The day after his announcement, thousands talked of their shock: 'But he looks so well!' When I found out that Tim was in Byron, I sent a message to his publicist. The next afternoon, in that hotter-than-normal August in Byron Bay, Tim called me, and we talked.

I was lying on my bed, heat-wrecked and very tired. The overhead fan was turned to full blast and the blinds were closed and, as we talked, I wondered what Tim was doing. I imagined he was sitting, his walking stick somewhere near, and maybe there was an ice pack on his head.

We talked about lots of things, including MS. I told him stuff I had never told anybody, and it felt good. I told him that some mornings I can't peel the foil lid from a plastic milk bottle, that I'm not able to walk up more than a single flight of stairs, how I have to drain my bladder, and sometimes manually evacuate my bowels – especially before a long drive, a lecture or festival gig, in case there's an 'accident' – and then, when there's any kind of heat, it all gets worse.

For more than a decade Tim toured the world with the Doug Anthony All Stars (DAAS) – the multi-award-winning comedy act – and he was known as 'the pretty one'. There'd be few people in Australia who don't know Tim Ferguson's name, and most in Sydney and Melbourne would recognize him in the street. When I was in my early twenties – and even though he isn't Jewish – I had a crush on him. I once queued up for an hour in the hope of scoring a ticket to one of his sell-out gigs.

Like me, for a long time, Tim told nobody he was sick. Unlike me, his illness is unpredictable, things stop working, he gets 'pins and needles' and his 'eyes go wonky' and his 'writing hand doesn't work so well' and then the symptoms disappear for a while, and sometimes come back even worse than they were before, or come back as different symptoms, some better, some more disabling.

Tim told me about numbness, blurred vision, falling out of bed, bouts of paralysis and not being able to dance 'with only one leg', which is his worst symptom, and the thing that brought touring with DAAS to a sudden end.

'When my hand's very bad,' I told him, 'I wear my bra to bed in case I can't fasten the clasp in the morning.'

I also told him how I drop things all the time, smash cups and plates, can't carry a packed suitcase, can't use the London Underground because of the heat and the stairs, and can't stand in a queue in the post office – or stand much at all.

It was very good to talk.

I didn't tell my boyfriend that I have MS until we'd been together for three months. I'd blamed not walking (and not moving much) on an ingrown toenail. I didn't make excuses for the other symptoms. We spent most of our time reading, writing, teaching and talking, and so my sluggish ways didn't seem strange.

In May 2010 we were in London for three days. On the third day I was in the Royal London and Barts for treatment. Trevor thought I'd been teaching a fiction workshop and when I got back to the hotel room he saw a bandage on my arm, which covered the place where the cannula had been. I'd forgotten to peel it off.

'What's that?' he said.

I told him about the bandage. I told him nearly everything.

That was more than two years ago, and we're together still. We have no children, but we've taught the voice-recognition software to swear, filled the house with portable fans, replaced the smashed crockery with melamine, and I've cancelled my pact with dying. ■

THE CUTTING

Rose Tremain

I could not for too long delay my promise to Violet Bathurst to cut out her Cancer.

Though I shied from the task, I knew that I had to discover in me some will to do it, before the Thing spread. For the thought of Violet dying alone in her dark chamber was a very sorrowful one. I do hold and believe that the deaths of those who have taken irrepressible pleasure in their moment-to-moment existence – in a world where many people seem sunk in a physical and spiritual twilight, or half-life – are to be especially mourned.

The Nurse I wanted to help with the Cutting was one Mrs McKinley, a bonny and kind Irishwoman, whose Catholic family had fled to England after the Protestant Settlements in Ireland in 1641. Mrs McKinley, now in her fifties and grown a little stout, had the gentlest, surest hands I have ever beheld in all my work with Nurses. More than this, her voice is of a great sweetness of tone and this, I have often observed, brings comfort to the Patient.

It also offers to me an accompaniment of amusement as I work, for that, in her Donegal accent, she addresses me not as Sir Robert, but as 'Sir Rabbit', and no matter how many times she says this, it always brings a smile to my lips and thus, though my fingers may be in a tangle of flesh and gore, I am afforded enough Lightness of Heart to be able to carry on.

To buy Opium for Violet, I first had to visit my most favoured Apothecary, Mr Dunn, in Norwich, a member of the Worshipful Society of the Art and Mystery of Apothecaries.

Of this designation the King had observed that the word 'mystery' appeared to him to be 'an inconvenient noun', which should not belong there.

'One does not wish there to be any *mystery* in the matter,' he pointed out. 'One wishes, on the contrary, that the Apothecary's knowledge be proven, or at least theoretical, as opposed to hypothetical, let alone mired in the Unknown. Is this not so, Merivel?'

I agreed that it was. The King then announced that he would be interested to talk to Mr Dunn and to inspect his premises. We thus travelled to Norwich together in the King's coach, and by the time we got there a great press of people, recognizing the King's Livery on his coachmen, had surrounded us.

I descended first and savoured the disappointment on the faces of the Crowd when they saw me (a mere Sir Rabbit) and not their Sovereign. But then I offered up my hand, and the King took it and descended in elegant style, notwithstanding the little limp that the obstinate Sore on his left leg has given him, and a great cry of rejoicing went up from the people assembled, and they reached out to try to touch the King, and a woman passed him her baby to hold in his arms.

I could see Mr Dunn, standing at the door of his Apothecary's Shoppe. I had not been able to give him any warning about the King's arrival, and when Dunn caught sight of his Sovereign, his body began to jerk in spasms of incredulity. He took off his Spectacles and put them on again, fearing his eyes were deceiving him. Then, suddenly bethinking himself of how he appeared, he cavorted into his Shoppe to remove his Wig and replace it with a better one.

Some time passed before we could make our way inside the Shoppe. Still holding the baby, the King embarked upon numerous conversations with the Crowd, enquiring after the Wool Trade in Norfolk and the Herring Fleets, and hearing how, in all honesty, the times were not very good 'for that people go short of money, Sir, after the hard winter storms, when the Fleets could not put out' and when 'many sheep had their breath frozen in their gullets by the ice and snow'.

I saw that the King listened attentively to these tales of dead sheep and unfished herrings, but offered no remedy. All he could find to say was: 'You must hold on. You people of Norfolk are stubborn and true. We are in May weather now. Better days are coming. You must hold on.'

When he said this, one man, a poor Fisherman, barged his way through the press of citizens to show the King his naked ribcage, which was so scantily clad with flesh, it could only put me in mind of Pearce's body just before he died. The man beat upon his ribs with his fists and cried out: 'I'm a beggar in Norwich now, Sir! Look at me! I had a Herring Boat at Yarmouth, but it was lost in the January tides and all my livelihood with it. And I have five children. Tell me how I am to "hold on"!'

At this the King passed the baby back to its mother and turned to me, snapped his fingers and said: 'Coins, Merivel! Give this poor Fellow a shilling or a half-crown immediately.' Then, as I scrabbled in my pockets for my Purse, he said to the Fisherman, 'Sudden loss is part of Life, as I, who lost my Father so cruelly, know well. And all we can do is to bear it. But here . . . here is kind Sir Robert Merivel, who will furnish you with a shilling or two, and tonight you and your family will eat your fill.'

Hands reached out to me – not only the filthy hand of the Fisherman-Beggar – and in less than one minute I was obliged to part with every bit of money that I had, for in a Crowd you cannot give to one and ignore the rest. The reaching out to me for coins only ended when I turned my purse inside out, to show that I had not one penny more to give. Nobody thanked me. And when at last we were able to turn and walk into Mr Dunn's premises, the King did not seem to have absorbed the fact that now I had no Means with which to buy the Opium I needed for Violet's Cutting. All he said was: 'I do not like it when I am face to face with Poverty and Want.'

Suspended from the ceiling in Mr Dunn's Shoppe is a strange variety of Stuffed Creatures: an Alligator, a Turtle, an Eel and a brace of Toads.

When you enter here, the slight stench from these Exhibits, which have hung there for a goodly time, might incline you to turn and walk out again, and I saw the King's nostrils dilate, and he produced from his sleeve a handkerchief scented with Lavender Water and held it to his nose awhile.

Then the scientific curiosity, which impelled him to start his own Laboratory at Whitehall and to give a Royal Charter to the Society for the Improvement of Natural Knowledge by Experiment, led him to forget any bodily inconvenience. He began to pick his careful way around Dunn's dark emporium, noting what the jars and galley pots and gourds contained, and setting aside his handkerchief to sniff at them. Then he suddenly turned to the Apothecary and asked: 'Where did you acquire your knowledge, Dunn? Was it properly come by?'

Adjusting his wig, Dunn stammered out that he had been apprenticed to an Apothecary as a boy of sixteen and, being 'both curious and reckless', had tried very many types of Physick on himself, 'to see what they would do to me . . .'

'How interesting,' said the King. 'Curiosity and recklessness may both be fine attributes in a man. I have often thought it.'

'Well, and in this way, Your Majesty,' said Dunn, stammering no more, 'when the Physicians prescribe, I can sometimes make a Correction, for that I have kept a Notebook of everything I tried, with all the quantities and manifestations of symptoms, and special notice of all the False Cures.'

'False Cures?'

'Sir Robert knows', said Dunn, 'the quantity of Mountebanks in this country! They will sell anything, Sir, call it "a Beautiful and Efficacious Vomit", say, and sell no matter what for a shilling and sixpence. It might be Rat Poison. It might nearly kill you. But some Physicians, they scarcely know what preparation does what to what, so then the Apothecary's knowledge, if it can, must be the Corrective to a False Cure.'

The King nodded approvingly. '*Nullius in verba*,' he said quietly. 'The Motto I gave to the Royal Society. *Take no man's word for it.* All should be done by proper experimentation. And you, Mr Dunn, seem to have followed this dictum admirably, by testing Compounds on yourself, though I warrant you may have got near to dying for it!'

'Well, I did, Sir. More than once. But here I am, alive. And what I like about my Trade is that there is no end to Medical Knowledge. Sir Robert, here, has taught me many things I did not know before.'

The King looked at me in mild astonishment. 'Has he? Has he really?'

'Many things.'

'Really? We know him chiefly as a Jester. A Jester and a Friend. But would you say he is a Good Physician?'

'Very good, Your Majesty.'

'Ah. How interesting. He once achieved a miraculous cure upon a favourite dog of mine, did you not, Merivel? But I think this was a Cure by Neglect, was it not?'

'Well, I would prefer to call it a Cure by Nature, Your Majesty. As the Great Fabricius said: "*Non dimenticare la Natura.*" I merely gave Nature time to work.'

'While you drank some fine Alicante and ate some figs and slept . . .'

'Only in order to *pass* the time.'

'Ha! You see, Dunn, why we love this man. He keeps laughter alive. But now to our main Business. We need a plentiful supply of Opium and neither of us has any money, for we have given it all away to poor Fisherfolk and the like. Will you accept the King's Credit?'

I wished to work upon my Cutting of Violet's Cancer in bright daylight, so that I could properly see what I was doing. I rode to Bathurst Hall and told her that I would come early on the morrow, and commanded her to have her bed removed nearer to the window.

'Mrs McKinley will accompany me,' I said, 'and I have stocked my bag with a great Quantity of Opium, so you will not feel any pain.'

Violet was sitting quietly in her *Salon* that day, doing Needlework, and finding her thus occupied cast me into gloom, for that I had never seen Violet Bathurst taken up by so static and conventional a Pastime.

'Violet,' I said, 'it hurts my soul to see you doing that. Pray let us have no more Embroidery once your Cancer is taken out!'

She raised her head and gazed at me sadly, holding out the work, which – unlike Celia's Needlework – was very inelegantly done, with bits and ends of thread hanging down in loops. 'Merivel,' she said, 'do not be so dense. Look what a novice I am. But I must learn to stitch in case, after the operation, it is *all* that I can do. Do you imagine that a woman with half a breast can play at Skittles?'

'Yes,' I said firmly. 'After a little Time of Recovery has passed. Indeed, I shall organize a party of Skittles at Bidnold and you can partner the King.'

Violet shook her head. 'You are dreaming,' she said. 'It will not come about.'

I rose early and collected Mrs McKinley from her house in Bidnold Village, and I noted how everything about her was clean and scrubbed, from her pink fingernails down to her polished boots.

I showed her the Opium I had got from Dunn and she said: 'Lord, Sir Rabbit, you could put an Army to sleep with this Quantity!' And an Image came to me of the Swiss Guards in the *Place d'Armes* at Versailles, lined up in their ranks, and then falling over in an Opium-induced trance, one by one. And I smiled.

'I am only anxious that Lady Bathurst does not suffer too much,' I said. 'But I warn you, she is much given to screaming, it is in her nature and you must try not to be too distracted by this.'

'No, no, Sir. I shall not be distracted. All my children were Screamers. I just shut my ears and said my prayers, and all went into a lovely Quietness.'

We arrived at Bathurst Hall and straight away were shown up to where Violet lay on her bed in its new position near the window. She looked very pale and the fierce easterly light etched lines on her skin that I had not noticed before. When I bent over her she reached up and pulled me towards her.

'Merivel,' she said, 'I am afraid . . .'

'It will be quick, Violet,' I said. 'In less than five minutes it will be over. We shall then stay by you while you sleep.'

I had commanded that a fire be lit in the room and a cauldron of water set on it to heat, and this had been done as I had asked. While I positioned a chair near the bed and prepared my Scalpel,

Mrs McKinley mixed a good quantity of the Opium powder with Brandy to make Laudanum and Violet swallowed this down. I watched her eyes flicker as it began to enter her blood.

Mrs McKinley then gently removed the top part of Violet's nightgown and took out clean muslin rags and washed the area of the Cutting in hot water and then with Tincture of Witch Hazel. After this she lifted Violet's arm and cleaned that also, saying, ''Twill be Nothing, My Lady. You will see. In a trice it will be gone.' With the cleaning done, she laid a square of linen under the arm, strapped Violet's wrists to the bedposts and begged her to stay as still as she was able.

At the door stood Violet's maid, Agatha, a pretty, dimpled girl, torn, I could see, between wanting to stay with her Mistress and desiring to flee. I turned to her and said: 'Agatha, go downstairs and heat a Warming Pan. The Shock of a Cutting can make a person very cold. I shall call to you when I want it brought here. Find woollen blankets and bring them too.'

The girl curtseyed and fled away. I looked over at Mrs McKinley.

'We shall give the Laudanum a little more time,' I said. 'Then we shall begin.'

Mrs McKinley pressed a white linen cap onto her head and rolled up her sleeves. She took Violet's hand in hers, gently stroking the palm. This stroking seemed to calm Violet, and we saw her eyes close and heard her breathing become deeper.

I raised the Scalpel. I told Mrs McKinley to press upon the breast, to draw the skin tight for the Cutting. As she did so, the Thing seemed to enlarge itself and I saw now that some small outcrop of it extended down into Violet's armpit, and this dismayed me, for I thought it would be a clean round Nub I was taking out, as if removing an eyeball from its socket. Now I understood that my Scalpel would have to make a second cut and then a third.

Mrs McKinley saw this too. 'I think 'tis more than it at first seemed, Sir Rabbit,' she whispered to me. 'Look there. And you will have to get it all.'

I took a breath. I cannot ever cut into another person's body without remembering how I had to hack deep into Katharine's body to deliver Margaret, and in consequence I remain calm, for I know that nothing could terrify me as profoundly as that operation did.

I made two swift cuts, like a cross, in the centre of the Cancer. Not much blood flowed. I lifted back the skin and investigated how deep I would have to go to bring out the lump of Cancerous matter, which was mottled purple and white in its colour and looked to me like some Sea Creature clinging to a rock pool.

Violet had begun to moan. Mrs McKinley spoke to her softly, telling her that the worst would soon be over.

I began the cutting. My blade went deep, circling the Cancer. Mrs McKinley dabbed at the flowing blood with her muslin rags. Violet began crying out in agony and her body arched and moved, so that my hand was jolted and the blade stabbed deeper than I had intended. Violet screamed. The scream was so loud and distressing to my head, it was as if Sound suddenly got in the way of Vision and blurred it. I blinked. With one hand Mrs McKinley was trying to hold Violet still and with the other swabbing blood from the wound.

'Try a prayer?' I hissed to Mrs McKinley.

'Oh, yes, a prayer. I will, Sir.'

She began a very low mumbling to God, asking Him to give us Quietness.

I blinked again and turned the Scalpel so that now I was cutting – or hoped I was – *underneath* the Cancer.

'I am almost there, Violet,' I said. 'I almost have it out . . .'

'No!' Violet cried. 'Let it alone! Close it up, Merivel. I can bear no more!'

'My Lady,' said Mrs McKinley, 'Sir Rabbit must take it all out, or it might grow again.'

'Let it grow!' cried Violet. 'I'm old and ugly now! Let it smother me and take me away with it!'

Mrs McKinley acted swiftly to pour more Laudanum into Violet's mouth and this – more than the prayer, I shall admit – quietened her.

I took up the muslin and swabbed and swabbed, to get the blood away. Then, probing with my finger, I felt the Cancer loosen from the flesh on one side. I cut again underneath and it loosened more. Blood ran over my hand.

Two more cuts and the Thing was loose. With my Spathomele I prised it out and set it in a glass dish. Pressing a wad of muslin hard on the wound, I stared at the Cancer and I thought how strange and terrible it was that the body, in its darkness and secrecy, produces Additions that can bring it to the grave.

Violet was quiet now, her breathing shallow. Dearly I wished that I could sew up the wound and there would be an end to the Cutting, but I knew that my labours were not done. In the armpit lay two Satellites of the main Cancer and these could not be left in Violet's body.

I took up the Scalpel again. I had promised that the whole Cutting would take no more than five minutes, but my struggles with the elusive Satellites took more than thirty-five, for they, it seemed, were welling over with blood and I could not cut without pausing while Mrs McKinley swabbed and swabbed.

By the time I came to sew up the skin, Violet was pale with deep shock and was hiccuping violently, and both Mrs McKinley and I began to fear she would be seized by Convulsions, or that her heart would cease.

Together we bandaged the wounds, then we cleaned our hands and arms with black Soap in hot water, and I called for Agatha to bring the warming pan and the blankets. We untied Violet's wrists and laid her right arm by her side, but placed the left arm on the pillow, away from the wounds.

Mrs McKinley, touching Violet's forehead with her strong hands, whispered to me, 'Lord, Sir, but she is terrible cold . . .'

Agatha came in, and when she saw the bloody rags all around and her Mistress pale as a Ghost, and the Cancerous tumours in the dish, almost fainted clean away. I took the warming pan from her and wrapped a blanket round it, and told Agatha to bring more hot water and bowls of Chocolate for me and Mrs McKinley.

Both the square of linen and the sheet underneath Violet were crimson and damp with blood, and Mrs McKinley and I knew that we had to get them away. But here was a difficult task, for the pain of movement would be very great for Violet. I put my arm under her right shoulder and neck, and lifted her forward, and Mrs McKinley peeled back the linen and the bloody sheet, then I laid her down again and raised her back and her buttocks, so that the sheet could come out. Then we spread out clean linen and pressed soft Pillows around the wound, and began to try to get her warm, setting the warming pan near her feet and covering her with the woollen blankets.

Into her mouth Mrs McKinley dribbled yet more Laudanum. The hiccups continued for another ten minutes. Then they stopped and Violet lay still and quiet before us. I lifted her wrist and felt for a pulse, and got it, faint, but ticking there, as the morning began slowly to pass.

Mrs McKinley took off her white cap and wiped her brow with it. 'Lord, Sir Rabbit,' she said, 'the Chocolate will be a lovely thing.'

We sat out all the daylight hours in Violet's room. The sun glanced on us, then hid itself behind cloud and the room darkened, as if promising rain.

My mind kept wandering to Bidnold and what the King and Margaret might be doing there, but I tried to put these ugly thoughts away. I knew that I had to remain with Violet until the morrow.

I watched her face, once almost beloved to me. She snored in her Laudanum sleep. I said in a low voice to Mrs McKinley, 'It was not done as cleanly as I had hoped.'

'Well,' she said, 'it was as difficult as any I've seen, including my own.'

'You had a Cancer in your breast?'

'I did. But it was cut out of me long ago, before I met you. And look at me, Sir Rabbit. Strong as a horse. I shall die ancient in my bed. You can lay a fat Wager on it.' ■

NIGHT

Alice Munro

When I was young, there seemed to be never a childbirth, or a burst appendix, or any other drastic physical event that did not occur simultaneously with a snowstorm. The roads would be closed, there was no question of digging out a car anyway, and some horses had to be hitched up to make their way into town to the hospital. It was just lucky that there were horses still around – in the normal course of events they would have been given up, but the war and gas rationing had changed all that, at least for the time being.

When the pain in my side struck, therefore, it had to do so at about eleven o'clock at night, and a blizzard had to be blowing, and since we were not stabling any horses at the moment, the neighbours' team had to be brought into action to take me to the hospital. A trip of no more than a mile and a half but an adventure all the same. The doctor was waiting, and to nobody's surprise he prepared to take out my appendix.

Did more appendixes have to be taken out then? I know it still happens, and it is necessary – I even know of somebody who died because it did not happen soon enough – but as I remember it was a kind of rite that quite a few people my age had to undergo, not in large numbers by any means but not all that unexpectedly, and perhaps not all that unhappily because it meant a holiday from school and it gave you some kind of status – set you apart, briefly, as one touched by the wing of mortality, all at a time in your life when that could be gratifying.

So I lay, minus my appendix, for some days, looking out a hospital window at the snow sifting in a sombre way through some evergreens. I don't suppose it ever crossed my head to wonder how my father was going to pay for this distinction. (I think he sold a woodlot that he had kept when he disposed of his father's farm, hoping to use it for trapping or sugaring or perhaps out of unmentionable nostalgia.)

Then I went back to school, and enjoyed being excused from physical training for longer than necessary, and one Saturday morning when my mother and I were alone in the kitchen she told me that my appendix had been taken out in the hospital, just as I thought, but it was not the only thing removed. The doctor had seen fit to take it out while he was at it, but the main thing that concerned him was a growth. A growth, my mother said, the size of a turkey's egg.

But don't worry, she said, it was all over now.

The thought of cancer never entered my head and she never mentioned it. I don't think there could be such a revelation today without some kind of question, some probing about whether it was or it wasn't. Cancerous or benign – we would want to know at once. The only way I can explain our failure to speak of it was that there must have been a cloud around that word like the cloud around the mention of sex. Worse, even. Sex was disgusting but there must be some gratification there – indeed we knew there was, though our mothers were not aware of it – while even the word cancer made you think of some dark, rotting, ill-smelling creature that you would not look at even when you kicked it out of the way.

So I did not ask and wasn't told and can only suppose it was benign or was most skilfully got rid of, for here I am today. And so little do I think of it that all through my life when called upon to list my surgeries, I automatically say or write only 'Appendix'.

This conversation with my mother would probably have taken place in the Easter holidays, when all the snowstorms, the snow-mountains, had vanished and the creeks were in flood, laying hold of anything they could get at, and the brazen summer just looming ahead. Our climate had no dallying, no mercies.

In the heat of early June I got out of school, having made good enough marks to free me from the final examinations. I looked well, I did chores around the house, I read books as usual, nobody knew there was a thing the matter with me.

Now I have to describe the sleeping arrangements in the bedroom occupied by my sister and me. It was a small room that could not accommodate two single beds, side by side, so the solution was a bunk bed, with a ladder in place to help whoever slept in the top bunk climb into bed. That was me. When I had been younger and prone to teasing, I would lift up the corner of my thin mattress and threaten to spit on my little sister lying helpless in the bunk below. Of course my sister – her name was Catherine – was not really helpless. She could hide under her covers, but my game was to watch until suffocation or curiosity drove her out, and at that moment to spit or successfully pretend to spit on her bared face, enraging her.

I was too old for such fooling, certainly too old now. My sister was nine when I was fourteen. The relationship between us was always unsettled. When I wasn't tormenting her, teasing her in some asinine way, I would take on the role of sophisticated counsellor or hair-raising storyteller. I would dress her up in some of the old clothes that had been put away in my mother's hope chest, being too fine to be cut up for quilts and too worn and precious for anybody to wear. I would put my mother's old caked rouge and powder on her face and tell her how pretty she looked. She was pretty, without a doubt, though the face I put on her gave her the look of a freakish foreign doll.

I don't mean to say that I was entirely in control of her, or even that our lives were constantly intertwined. She had her own friends, her own games. These tended towards domesticity rather than glamour. Dolls were taken for walks in their baby carriages, or sometimes kittens were dressed up and walked in the dolls' stead, always frantic to get out. Also there were play sessions where somebody got to be the teacher and could slap the others over the wrists and make them pretend to cry, for various infractions and stupidities.

In the month of June, as I have said, I was free of school and left on my own, as I don't remember being in quite the same way at any other time of my growing up. I did some chores in the house, but my mother must have been well enough, as yet, to handle most of that work. Or perhaps we had just enough money at the time to hire what she – my mother – would call a maid, though everybody else said hired-girl. I don't remember, at any rate, having to tackle any of those jobs that piled up for me in later summers, when I fought quite willingly to maintain the decency of our house. It seems that the mysterious turkey egg must have given me some invalid status, so that I could spend part of the time wandering about like a visitor.

Though not trailing any special clouds. Nobody in our family would have got away with that. It was all inward – this uselessness and strangeness I felt. And not continual uselessness either. I remember squatting down to thin the baby carrots, as you had to do every spring. So the root would grow to a decent size to be eaten.

It must have been just that every moment of the day was not filled up with jobs, as it was in summers before and after.

So maybe that was the reason that I had begun to have trouble getting to sleep. At first, I think, that meant lying awake maybe till around midnight and wondering at how wide awake I was, with the rest of the household asleep. I would have read, and got tired in the usual way, and turned out my light and waited. Nobody would have called out to me earlier, telling me to put out my light and get to sleep. For the first time ever (and this too must have marked a special status) I was left to make up my own mind about such a thing.

It took a while for the house to change, from the light of day and then of the household lights turned on late in the evening, from the general clatter of things to be done, hung up, finished with, to a stranger place in which people and the work that dictated their lives fell away, their uses for everything around them fell away, all the furniture retreated into itself without wanting or needing any attention from you.

You might think this was liberation. At first, perhaps it was. The freedom. The strangeness. But as my failure to fall asleep prolonged itself and as it finally took hold altogether until it changed into the dawn, I became more and more disturbed. I started saying rhymes, then real poetry, first to make myself go under but then hardly of my own volition. But the activity seemed to mock me. I was mocking myself, as the words turned into absurdity, into the silliest random speech.

I was not myself.

I had been hearing that said of people now and then, all my life, without thinking what it could mean.

So who do you think you are, then?

I'd been hearing that too, without attaching to it any real menace, just taking it as a sort of routine jeering.

Think again.

By this time it wasn't sleep I was after. I knew mere sleep wasn't likely. Maybe not even desirable. Something was taking hold of me and it was my business, my hope, to fight it off. I had the sense to do that, but only barely, as it seemed. It was trying to tell me to do things, not exactly for any reason but just to see if such acts were possible. It was informing me that motives were not necessary.

It was only necessary to give in. How strange. Not out of revenge, or even cruelty, but just because you had thought of something.

And I did think of it. The more I chased the thought away, the more it came back. No vengeance, no hatred – as I've said, no reason, except that something like an utterly cold deep thought that was hardly an urging, more of a contemplation, could take possession of me. I must not even think of it but I did think of it.

The thought was there and hanging on to my mind. The thought that I could strangle my little sister, who was asleep in the bunk below me and whom I loved more than anybody in the world.

I might do it not for any jealousy, viciousness or anger, but because of madness, which could be lying right beside me there in the night. Not a savage madness either, but something that could be almost teasing. A lazy, teasing, half-sluggish suggestion that seemed to have been waiting a long time.

It might be saying why not? Why not try the worst?

The worst. Here in the most familiar place, the room where we had lain for all of our lives and thought ourselves most safe. I might do it for no reason I or anybody could understand, except that I could not help it.

The thing to do was to get up, to get myself out of that room and out of the house. I went down the rungs of the ladder and never cast a single look at my sister where she slept. Then quietly down the stairs, nobody stirring, into the kitchen where everything was so familiar to me that I could make my way without a light. The kitchen door was not really locked – I am not even sure that we possessed a key. A chair was pushed under the doorknob, so that anybody trying to get in would make a great clatter. A slow careful removal of the chair could be managed without making any noise at all.

After the first night I was able to make my moves without a break, so as to be outside within a couple of smooth seconds.

There. At first everything was black, because I would have lain wakeful for a long time, and the moon had already gone down. I kept on staying in bed as long as I thought I could for several nights, as if it was a defeat to have to give up trying to sleep, but after some time I got out of bed as a regular habit, as soon as the house seemed to be dreaming. And the moon of course had its own habits, so sometimes I stepped into a pool of silver.

Of course there were no street lights – we were too far from town.

Everything was larger. The trees around the house were always called by their names – the beech tree, the elm tree, the oak tree, the maples always spoken of in the plural and not differentiated, because they clung together. The white lilac tree and the purple lilac tree never referred to as bushes because they had grown too big. The front and back and side lawns were easy to negotiate because mowed by myself with the idea of giving us some town-like respectability. My mother had once had that idea too. She had planted a semicircular lawn past the lilac trees, and edged to with spirea bushes and delphinium plants. That was all gone now.

The east side of our house and the west side looked on two different worlds, or so it seemed to me. The east side was the town side, even though you could not see any town. Not more than two miles away there were houses in rows, with street lights and running water, and though, as I have said, you could not see any of that, I am really not sure that you couldn't get a faint glow if you stared long enough. To the west, the long curve of the river and the fields and the trees and the sunsets had nothing to interrupt them ever.

Back and forth I walked, first close to the house and then venturing here and there as I got to rely on my eyesight and could count on not bumping into the pump handle or the platform that supported the clothes line. The birds began to stir, and then to sing – as if each of them had thought of it separately, up there in the trees. They woke far earlier than I would have thought possible. But soon, soon after those earliest starting songs, there got to be a little whitening to the sky. And suddenly I was overwhelmed with sleepiness. I went back into the house, where there was suddenly darkness everywhere, and I very properly, carefully, silently, set the tilted chair under its knob, and went upstairs without a sound, managing doors and steps with the caution necessary although I seemed already half asleep. I fell into my pillow. And I woke late – late in our house being around nine o'clock.

I would remember everything then but it was so absurd – the bad part of it indeed was so absurd – that I could hardly bother about it. My brother and sister had gone off to school – being still in public school, they were not getting time off for good exam performances, as I was. When they got home in the afternoon my sister was somebody who could never have passed through such a danger. It was absurd. We swung together in the hammock, one of us at either end.

It was in that hammock that I spent much of the days, and that may have been the simple reason for my not getting to sleep at night. And since I did not speak of my night difficulties, nobody came up with the simple information that I'd be better to get more action during the daytime.

My troubles returned with the night, of course. The demons grabbed hold of me again. And in fact it got worse. I knew enough to get up and out of my bunk without any pretending that things would get better and I would go to sleep if I just tried hard enough. I made my way as carefully out of the house as I had done before. I became able to find my way around more easily; even the inside of those rooms became more visible to me and yet more strange. I could make out the tongue-in-groove kitchen ceiling put in when the house was built maybe a hundred years ago, and the northern window frame partly chewed away by a dog that had been shut in the house one night long before I was born. I remembered what I had completely forgotten – that I used to have a sandbox there, placed where my mother could watch me out the north window. A great bunch of golden glow was flowering in its place now, you could hardly see out of that window at all.

The east wall of the kitchen had no windows in it but it had a door opening on a stoop where we stood to hang out the heavy wet washing, and haul it in when it was dry and smelling fresh and triumphant, from white sheets to dark heavy overalls.

At that stoop I sometimes halted in my night walks. I never sat down but it eased me to look towards town, maybe just to inhale the sanity of it. All the people getting up before long, having their shops to go to, their doors to unlock and window arrangements to see to, their busyness.

One night – I can't say whether it was the twentieth or the twelfth or only the eighth or the ninth that I had got up and walked – I got a sense, too late for me to change my pace, that there was somebody around the corner. There was somebody waiting there and I could do nothing but walk right on. I would be caught if I turned back.

Who was it? Nobody but my father. He too was looking towards town and that improbably faint light. He was dressed in his day clothes – dark work pants, the next thing to overalls but not quite, and dark shirt and boots. He was smoking a cigarette. A roll-your-own, of course. Maybe the cigarette smoke had alerted me to another presence, though it's possible that in those days the smell of tobacco smoke was everywhere, inside and out.

He said good morning, in what might have seemed a natural way except that there was nothing natural about it. We weren't accustomed to giving such greetings in our family. There was nothing hostile about this – it was just thought unnecessary, I suppose, to give a greeting to somebody you would be seeing off and on all day long.

I said good morning back. And it must have really been getting towards morning or my father would not have been dressed for a day's work in that way. The sky may have been whitening but hidden still between the heavy trees. The birds singing, too. I had taken to staying away from my bunk till later and later, even though I didn't get comfort from doing that as I had at first. The possibilities that had once inhabited only the bedroom, the bunk beds, were taking up the corners everywhere.

Now that I come to think of it, why wasn't my father in his overalls? He was dressed as if he had to go into town for something, first thing in the morning.

I could not continue walking, the whole rhythm of it had been broken.

'Having trouble sleeping?' he said.

My impulse was to say no, but then I thought of the difficulties of explaining that I was just walking around, so I said yes.

He said that was often the case on summer nights.

'You go to bed tired out and then just as you think you're falling asleep you're wide awake. Isn't that the way?'

I said yes.

I knew now that he had not heard me getting up and walking around on just this one night. The person whose livestock was on the premises, whose earnings such as they were lay all close by, who kept a handgun in his desk drawer, was certainly going to stir at the slightest creeping on the stairs and the easiest turning of a knob.

I am not sure what conversation he meant to follow then, as regards my being awake. He had declared such wakefulness to be a nuisance. Was that to be all? I certainly did not intend to tell him more. If he had given the slightest intimation that he knew there was more, if he'd even hinted that he had come here intending to hear it, I don't think he'd have got anything out of me at all. I had to break the silence out of my own will, saying that I could not sleep. I had to get out of bed and walk.

Why was that?

I had dreams.

I don't know if he asked me, were those bad dreams?

We could take that for granted, I think.

He let me wait to go on, he didn't ask anything. I meant to back off but I kept talking. The truth was told with only the slightest modification.

When I spoke of my little sister I said that I was afraid I would hurt her. I believed that he would know what I meant. Kill. Not hurt. Kill, and for no reason. None at all. A possession.

There was no satisfaction, really, once I had got that out. I had to say it then. Kill her.

Now I could not unsay it, I could not go back to the person I had been before.

My father had heard it. He had heard that I thought myself capable – for no reason, capable – of strangling my little sister in her sleep. He said, 'Well.'

Then he said not to worry. He said, 'People have those kinds of thoughts sometimes.'

He said this quite seriously but without any sort of alarm or jumpy surprise. People have these kinds of thoughts or fears if you like, but there's no real worry about it, no more than a dream. Probably to do with the ether.

He did not say, specifically, that I was in no danger of doing any such thing. He seemed more to be taking it for granted that such a thing could not happen. An effect of the ether, he said. No more sense than a dream. It could not happen, in the way that a meteor could not hit our house (of course it could, but the likelihood of it doing so put it in the category of couldn't).

He did not blame me, though, for thinking of it.

There were other things he could have said. He could have questioned me further about my attitude to my little sister or my dissatisfactions with my life in general. If this were happening today, he might have made an appointment for me to see a psychiatrist. (I think that is what I might have done, a generation and an income further on.)

The fact is that what he did worked as well. It set me down, but without either mockery or alarm, in the world we were living in.

If you live long enough as a parent you discover that you have made mistakes you didn't bother to know about as well as the ones you do know about, all too well. You are somewhat humbled at heart, sometimes disgusted with yourself. I don't think my father felt anything like this. I do know that if I had ever taxed him, he might have said something about liking or lumping it. The encounters I had as a child with his belt or the razor strop. (Why do I say encounters? It's to show I'm not a howling sissy any more, I can make light.) Those strappings, then, would have stayed in his mind, if they stayed at all, as no more than quite adequate curbing of a mouthy child's imagining that she could rule the roost.

'You thought you were too smart,' was what he might have given as his reason, and indeed one heard that often in those times. Not always referring to myself. But a number of times, it did.

However, on that breaking morning he gave me just what I needed to hear and what I was to forget about, soon enough.

I have thought that he was maybe in his better work clothes because he had a morning appointment to go to the bank, and to learn there, not to his surprise, that there was no extension to his loan, he had worked as hard as he could but the market was not going to turn around and he had to find a new way of supporting us and paying off what we owed at the same time. Or he may have found out that there was a name for my mother's shakiness and that it was not going to stop. Or that he was in love with an impossible woman.

Never mind. From then on I could sleep. ■

The Lady and the Skull

The skull, picked quite clean
And bleached by the sun and wind
Until it is more an objet d'art
Than a memento mori
Is trying to speak to me.

In just such an emblematic a fashion
The world takes on
Human form. If it did not do so,
How could I understand it?
After a great deal of thought,
I reached the following conclusion –
The imperative study
Is that of the mute languages
Sign and cipher, the baulked speech
Of stones, implements and skeletons.
I believed I had defined the problem
With which the picked skull had presented me.
To define the problem is, is it not,
Halfway to solving it? To give
To the unnameable the name of unnameable is to name it as the
  unnameable. And so to fix it.
I remarked, in a conciliatory fashion, to the skull:
I know you are not death,
I am no maiden either.

First we must purify our imagery;
Then we can begin.

MY HEART

Semezdin Mehmedinović

TRANSLATED FROM THE BOSNIAN BY CELIA HAWKESWORTH

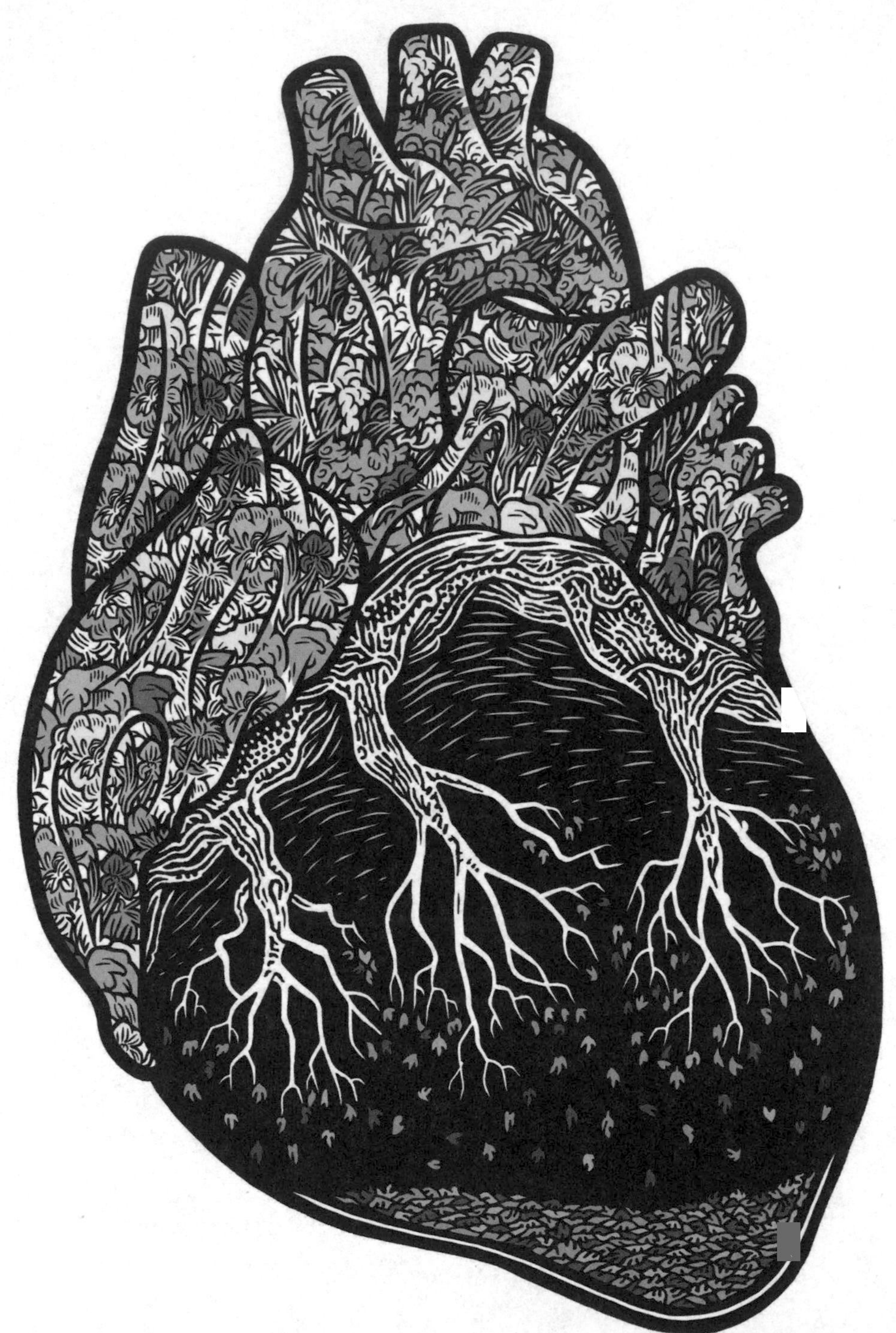

Today, it seems, was the day I was meant to die.

I was getting ready for work, taking a shower, when I felt a dull, metallic pain in my chest and throat, and the taste of cement on my tongue. I stepped out of the shower with a feeling of indescribable fatigue and wrapped my wet body in a bathrobe. Sanja was just about to leave the apartment to go to work, but then she caught sight of me through the open bathroom door. I told her I wasn't feeling well, I was going back to bed for a bit, this *weariness* would soon pass, and she shouldn't hesitate to go.

She stayed. Wet, my hair dripping, wrapped in the bathrobe, I stretched out on the bed. And I felt increasingly worse. She brought me cold tea, which didn't help, and then, having no choice, she called 911. After that, she stared out at the street impatiently, looking for the ambulance. I didn't have the energy to turn onto my other side to watch her by the window. I looked at the sofa where she had been sitting. I felt suddenly uneasy because she wasn't where she had just been. Then I looked at the photograph on the wall above the sofa . . .

Llasa. Early morning. A young Buddhist priest in a red robe had come out through a high wooden door in the wall of a stone building, and was now walking down a narrow cobbled lane, with a wisp of morning mist in front of him – a small white cloud, like a ghost that the priest was following. I let my gaze follow the white cloud above the cobblestones in Tibet.

Behind me, Sanja said: 'Here they are.' Then she came back into my field of vision. She opened the door and looked down the corridor, then anxiously glanced back towards me. And then our room was filled with strangers from the emergency services, settling themselves briskly around me on the sofa. I had never experienced such an aggressive assault on my privacy. Quite uninhibited and sure of themselves, they looked around the room, glanced at me, admired the floral pattern of the coverlet I was lying on; strangers in my room. A girl in a blue uniform had just opened my bathrobe, so that I lay before them naked, and asked: 'How old are you, sir?'

'Fifty.'

After the initial shock, there was peace.

I looked at everything around me without emotion, and so – without fear. And now that it is over, I remember the event as though I had seen it from a distance, just as though my mind had become separate from my body and had observed what was going on almost with indifference.

The shock did not come when the girl in the blue uniform said: 'Sir, you're having a heart attack!'

That's when I felt calm. In films, when they are describing a critical state such as this, the picture is often left without sound, and sometimes they even make it slow motion. That is a technical evocation of the mind at work.

The mind behaves like a cold camera lens.

In my case, the shock had come at the moment when the ambulance arrived, especially when a bunch of strangers filled my room. This was something that happened to other people, not to me, and it was something I recoiled from. And here my fear of illness was expressed as fear of doctors and hospitals. I never went to hospitals, even as a visitor. And now, the girl in the blue uniform leaned over me on my sofa, and said: 'You're having a heart attack!'

My first thought: She's wrong, this isn't my heart. Then I thought: I know this girl from somewhere. I tried to remember where from, but now there were a lot of human hands above me, attaching me to wires, turning me to the left, then to the right, disturbing my train of thought. I could not remember where I had seen that girl before. Through her blue blouse, I saw the outline of her breasts, but did not recognize it in any way sexual. She was looking at me anxiously, as though accusing me of something.

And one other optical impression: the bodies of all those people around me were unnaturally big, while my body had shrunk. What was it I was feeling? Weariness. Weariness from the pressure in my chest, which was making me breathless, which had become the same as weariness with life. And I thought: So, is this it? Is this death? At that moment, in fact, I began to see everything not just as a participant, but also as an outside observer. And I thought: It's good, just let it all pass, I'm tired, I want to close my eyes and not remember. I want it all to stop.

The years I had lived through up to now were already too much.

On the way to the hospital, lying in the ambulance, my knee crushed by the weight of an oxygen canister, I watched the passing clouds, the green traffic signals that I had noticed up to then only as a driver. Through the back door of the ambulance, after we slowed down for something, I saw a sign on the facade of a brick building with the inscription LIBERATION BOOKS.

'What's the name of this street?' I asked the girl in the blue uniform leaning over me to fix my headrest.

Was my mind turning anywhere, just to forget the pain in my chest? The young man sitting by my feet kept shifting the heavy metal canister that was lying on my legs. He shifted it so that the cold metal lay uncomfortably against the bone of my knee, and for a while that became the dominant pain in my body. That made me silently furious with the young man, who was, perhaps, scraping the oxygen canister against my knees on purpose, intending to deflect my mind away from my heart to a different problem.

Then I turned my attention to the tops of the trees lining the street. In the autumn, the leaves here take on such dazzling, sunny colours that even on a cloudy day one has the impression of a surplus of light. Was it a sunny morning? Or did the colours in the treetops give me an illusion of sun? I had always been disturbed by the thought of dying in a landscape where deciduous trees grew. There was something unconvincing, something *obvious* about that.

It was somehow indecent to die in the autumn.

It was kitsch to die in the autumn, along with everything else.

The ambulance stopped in front of the hospital. In the parking lot, the first image I saw from my horizontal position was this: walking between the cars towards the hospital building was a girl in the red hockey shirt of the Washington Capitals. She was looking up, towards a window, or at a cloud.

I had only ever been in this parking lot once before, when the wife of the poet F. was giving birth to their daughter. I remember that he had bought a new Toyota Camry that day, and asked me: 'Would you like to drive it?' 'Sure.' And I drove once round the parking lot. That was ten years ago. I can still remember the smell of the new car.

My oxygen mask began to mist up in the icy November air.

At the hospital entrance, I was met by a choir of smiling medical personnel. On my right, a nurse struggled to find a vein in my arm to take blood. On my left, two girls in green coats gazed and marvelled at the design of the coverlet I was wrapped in. At the same time, I caught sight of Sanja at the end of the corridor; a man (a doctor?) had just come up to her with some papers in his hand. She listened carefully to what he said and then began to cry.

The man was now leaning over me. He felt my pulse with cold fingers and asked: 'How old are you?'

'Fifty.'

I want to go back to my apartment for a moment.

What is the answer to the question *Who am I?* while strangers are examining my naked body in my own room? And among them is that girl I know from somewhere. What fills me with unease and muffled shame is not the proximity of death, but the realization that my body, at this moment, is an object without emanations. My corporality is asexual.

What is more, the ease with which these strangers shift my body through space creates an impression of my own weightlessness. I am what is left over of me, my mortal remains, as I lie in my bathrobe, under which I am naked.

All I know about the body I know as a poet, and that is pretty selective, limited to those characteristics in which the body displays its abilities and strength, and not its weaknesses and shortcomings.

About the diseases of the body, I actually know nothing.

The mind draws logical conclusions on the basis of data accessible to it, and when the attack happened, while I was standing under the shower in the bathroom, I immediately connected the pain in my throat and metal taste in my mouth with an article I had read in *Vanity Fair*. It was an account of an attack experienced by the author (Christopher Hitchens, who was later diagnosed with cancer). In that description he says that he felt pain in his chest and neck, and felt something like 'the slow drying of cement' in his chest (I'm quoting this from memory, but I think those were the words he used to describe his state, which was what I was now experiencing). And when I came out of the shower, and the pain in my chest increased, I was convinced that I had cancer.

Later, the emergency services arrived, and the girl (a doctor in a blue uniform) leaned over me and said: 'Sir, you are having a heart attack!' And my first thought had been: No, dear. This can't be my heart.

My mind was so firmly convinced that my symptoms were like those in the description of Hitchens's attack that I favoured the account from his article over the official diagnosis. In any case, at one moment I thought: This is comical! I'm dying thinking about Christopher Hitchens!

It was comical: my reality, at such a crucial moment, was being explained by a columnist in *Vanity Fair*, who did not know I existed, and so could not know, either, that I was, perhaps, right now ceasing to exist.

'How old are you?'
'Fifty.'

This was a dialogue that kept being repeated today.

The number of years I had lived represented important information for the doctors. I had the feeling that, in this way, for the first time – in this long life – my time was being accurately measured. This meant that today all my illusions of youth vanished. We rationalize our experience of time, but beyond the givens of the calendar, we are not conscious of it. Because 'in spirit' we stay the same. 'In spirit' I was the same person I had been in my twenties. That's how it is, probably, with everyone; it is a characteristic of our species. That is how we protect ourselves from death. Western cultures see man in his asymmetry and disharmony, so they separate him into a body that ages, and a soul that does not age. Apart, presumably, from Dostoevsky.

Reduced to a body lying on the operating table, I communicated the whole time with my eyes and through a meagre exchange of words with various people who were working on my revival. This was a surprising number of people – those who prepared for the operation, and those who participated in it. They all struck up conversations with the dying person, and my impression was that the body (i.e. me) did not offer much information, even on the operating table. Apart from my unpronounceable name, the only piece of information about me was this coverlet with the floral pattern à la Paul Gauguin, in which I was wrapped when I came here; everyone commented on it, interested in the cultural origin of the drawing on canvas, presumably convinced that the coverlet had the same geographical origin as me.

At one point the surgeon who was operating on me, not knowing how to negotiate my complicated name, brought his face close to mine and explained, slightly alarmed, that he would have to communicate with me in the course of the operation and for that communication he would need a name to call me by. He said: 'I'll call you Me'med. Is that all right?'

As for the coverlet, I don't know exactly where it came from, other than that it was some South American country. Perhaps from the same country as one of the hospital staff who took such an interest in it. In any case, these people treated my origin with great sensitivity, although they did not ask, nor, I presume, did they know where I came from. From my accent they knew only that I was foreign.

Does this mean that we all suffer from a kind of anxiety about dying in a distant, foreign country, a world where we are not at home?

This is the first time I see inside my body. On the left of the operating table there is a screen on which is projected an image of my cardiac arteries. What I see reminds me of a branching plant. One very thin, almost transparent twig had begun to grow and lengthen. Behind that *growth* was an unknown, delicate procedure that the doctor applied to my blocked artery, so as to break through the blockage and enable the normal flow of blood. Instantly, I felt indescribable relief. The same procedure was applied to the other artery: I watched as the branch grew before my eyes.

And that was all. The pain in my throat and pressure in my chest disappeared. The moment of liberated breathing was so refreshing that all trace of tiredness left my body. This made me want to straighten up, to get off the operating table and walk.

Full of oxygen.

The theatre unexpectedly emptied, and for a short time I was alone. I heard a buzzing but didn't know what was making the sound. A machine?

Then the room filled up with human voices again. None of them took any notice of me. They were discussing the previous night's episode of a television series.

And they were laughing.

One girl, an African American, leaned over me and asked: 'Would you like me to bring some water?' A Latino lad came after her and, as though it were part of an ongoing conversation with her, said: 'You must!'

I said: 'Yes, please.'

And she answered him: 'I can't. I won't!'

Someone else in the room was describing how he had spent half an hour that morning stuck in a lift. Finally the person responsible for the lift had appeared, and when they had freed him, he felt, he said, 'like a Chilean miner who had just been brought out of the earth into the sun'.

I drank water out of a plastic cup. And I couldn't remember when I was last that aware of the taste of ordinary, sweet water.

From the operating theatre, lying on a narrow trolley, I went by lift to the ward. I was accompanied by two young people in hospital coats who didn't seem to be in a hurry to go anywhere; they were talking, laughing, and easily forgot my presence. They could have been lovers. Beside them, I felt my primary characteristics returning to my body. When we entered the lift, it turned out that my height in a horizontal position was such that they had trouble fitting me into the moving box of the lift. And when the doors closed, I could feel them rubbing against my feet as we moved.

All the people I meet today disappear. They vanish without my having a chance to say goodbye. These two young lovers who had been chirruping and laughing in the lift, as they took me from the lower to the upper floors, they too went away without my noticing the moment of their departure.

In my ward, a new nurse settled me in the bed and said: 'Lovely coverlet.'

I said I had brought it from home. She explained that I could by all means keep it here as well. Maybe she believed I had a childish emotional attachment to that rug.

Then I called Sanja, who had got lost somewhere in the depressing architecture of the hospital corridors.

If a line is drawn under Tuesday, the 2nd of November, 2010, this is what happened to me:

As I was getting ready to go to work, I had a heart attack.

I was in the shower when I felt a dull, metallic pressure in my chest and throat, and when, soon afterwards, the ambulance arrived, the girl who examined me said, bluntly and without beating about the bush: 'You're having a heart attack.' Under an oxygen mask, I watched Sanja on the sofa opposite the bed where I was lying surrounded by strangers. Her face was contorted with fear. They hurried to take me away, wrapped in the cover on which I was lying; they took me to hospital, and then I had an operation. And after they had installed stents in my blocked arteries, I was settled into a hospital ward. It all took a little more than three hours, but during that time my world was fundamentally altered.

After the operation, the doctor looked for Sanja, but she was not in the waiting room. When they had put me into the ward, I called her on her mobile. She answered, she was on her way. She came into the room, pale as pale, her face swollen with crying. That face expressed uncontrolled joy and an absolute sadness that had overwhelmed her. Something in her was broken. She had an irresistible urge to hug me, but didn't dare for fear that an embrace might hurt. I asked her to sit on the bed, beside me.

'Where were you?'

'Outside the hospital.'

'It's cold outside, and you're dressed like *that* . . .' I'd only just noticed that – in her haste – she had just put a little jumper on over her T-shirt.

'I didn't dare wait.'

'What do you mean?'

'I was afraid the doctor was going to come and tell me . . .'

'Tell you what?'

'. . . that you'd died.'

'It hadn't quite come to that.'

'When I was giving them permission to operate, they asked – did I want them to fetch a priest?'

'What did you say?'

'I said there was no need for that, and that you weren't going to die.'

'You didn't tell them that a priest couldn't reconcile me to God . . .'

'No.'

'You should have!' I said, joking.

She pretended to be cross (people were dying here and he was having a laugh!), then she slapped me gently with her open hand on my chest, then at the same instant remembered my heart and shuddered, she could have hurt me oh oh oh, she waved her hands in the air over me ohohohooo. Then we laughed.

I remember the rest of the day quite clearly as well.

When I was left alone in the ward, this is what I thought about:

Of course I had been thinking and all these years I had been developing my attitude towards my death, but I did not expect that it could come as a consequence of my heart stopping. All my other organs could stop functioning, but the heart was out of the question. It was here, I thought, to beat for me, just as long as I needed it.

I called my son Harun. He was now in St Louis. At the airport.

'How long is it till your flight?'

'Six hours.'

At midnight on 31 January 1996, on our way from Zagreb to Phoenix, Arizona, on our émigré journey to America, we had been at St Louis Airport.

We were changing planes.

I remember rows of grey leather seats in the waiting room, and midnight travellers with Stetsons. In those days there were ashtrays on high stands beside the seats, and the stale air reeked of Jack Daniel's. There wouldn't be any ashtrays there any more. And now, as I chatted to him, I remembered a photograph from that journey. It was of him asleep, his head resting on his arms on a table in the airport cafe. He was thirteen then. I was thirty-five. He's twenty-eight now. Almost as old as I was that midnight, when we were wearily waiting for the plane to Phoenix. How long ago was that? Fifteen years.

'I'm sorry, son.'

'What for?'

'That you've got such a long wait.'

'You're comforting me, as though I was the one who'd had his heart stitched up!'

That *textile* image 'stitched up' surprised me. As I thought about it, language became the only reality. I felt that every physical touch was freed of pain, and that was a nice illusion.

I'm really well, I feel cheerful and it's easy to forget I've had my heart 'stitched up'.

Other than a dull ache in the vein they opened in my groin: in that soft area between my genitals and my thigh.

When I was lying on the operating table, at a certain moment I became conscious of that, that they were shaving my groin; a cold and quite disagreeable touch. At the time I didn't know why they were doing that. If my problem is my heart, I thought, why are they shaving my private parts?

A cold razor blade scraping over my skin.

And the image of a man condemned to death, being prepared in the morning for the electric chair, came suddenly to my mind.

And then this. Today Sanja said that was it. No more cigarettes. 'If you want to go on living,' she said, 'you have to stop.'

And it was high time.

'There's a Bosnian, a doctor in Kentucky. I heard this story today. He had a heart attack, just like you, and while he was still in hospital, he asked his wife to park the car behind the hospital building. Then he'd go out, hide in the car and smoke a cigarette. Imagine! A doctor. His unfortunate wife refused to bring cigarettes, and she told his doctor colleagues about it.'

In America everything is geared to stopping you smoking. Of all the nations on the planet, they are the most resistant to the tobacco habit.

Nevertheless, one of the finest sentences about the cigarette and dependence on it was written by an American, Laird Hunt:

When you smoke, other people come up to you and ask for a light.

The next day.

I thought about how the news of her son's heart attack could affect my mother in Bosnia. In order to pre-empt any possible pain, I called her and explained that a rumour that I had had a heart attack was likely to spread through the Bosnian part of the world. I was calling, I said, so that my voice and cheerfulness would reassure her that this was not the case. She listened to me attentively, then there was a short pause before she asked: 'So, how are you, otherwise?'

I clearly recognized her anxiety in that *otherwise*.

'Of all possible diseases, they hit on a heart attack,' she said. 'The Mehmedinovićes don't have them. No one in our family either on your father's side or on mine has ever had a problem with their heart.'

So, that meant I was the first. Genetic degeneration had to start with someone; or else I – like all my relations – started out with the same heart, only I had carelessly filled mine with stuff that exceeded its capacity.

And when the call was over, I remembered a line of verse that I had last thought about perhaps in the late 1970s. It wasn't remotely worthy, metaphysical poetry, but a rudimentary line by the forgotten Bosnian poet Vladimir Nastić that went:

I nearly swooned, Mother, like you, giving birth to me.

Sanja came this morning before eight o'clock. On her way to the ward, she had bought me a decaf in the hospital canteen. The decaf was sweetened with artificial sweetener.

It wasn't coffee, it wasn't sugar, nor was I myself.

And she said: 'You're looking well!'

I nodded affirmatively. Clearly I looked well, tied to the bed with all these cables so that I couldn't move, or sit up, or get out of bed and walk around the room. But that didn't bother me. I drank the coffee with great pleasure, just as though it was real coffee, with natural white sugar.

This morning a new nurse came. She said that it would be good for me to move, to walk around the room. I instantly dug myself out of bed, still plugged into hundreds of wires and with needles in my veins.

In the bathroom, Sanja carefully washed my whole body with a wet cloth.

Then I walked around the room. It was good to be walking again. This was what the experience of one's first step was like. I was walking!

But afterwards, I was sitting in my chair and suddenly straightened up, and at that moment I felt something burst in my right groin (where they had shaved my private parts the day before with a razor). At the same moment I saw a swelling appear. I pressed the button on my bed to call the nurse, who came quickly, and looked at the swelling with interest. She measured my penis, which was lying over the swelling, against the outside edge of her hand. She was concerned. She measured the pulse in my feet and hurried out of the room to find the duty doctor.

Very soon, instead of her or the doctor, a young man appeared, a technician with a strange plastic object. In the centre of the square object there was a half ball, which he pressed onto the swelling. The ends of the surface into which the ball was set had holes with a paper string drawn through them. He tied the string round my waist. But he moved slowly, all the time reading the instructions for installing this plastic object whose purpose was, presumably, to read impulses, or messages sent by the swelling near my genitals.

And it wasn't working.

He gave up.

He laid the plastic object down on the bedside cabinet, and left.

Was I now supposed to act like someone ill?

I didn't want to.

No.

In Chekhov's diaries there is a short note, a sketch for a

story, about a man who went to the doctor, who examined him and discovered a weakness in his heart.

After that the man changed the way he lived, took medicines and talked obsessively about his weakness; the whole town knew about his heart, and all the town's doctors (whom he consulted regularly) talked about his illness. He did not marry, he stopped drinking, he always walked slowly and breathed with difficulty.

Eleven years later, he travelled to Moscow and went to see a cardiologist. That was how it emerged that his heart was, in fact, in excellent shape. To begin with, he was overjoyed at his health. But it quickly turned out that he was unable to return to a normal way of life, as he was completely adapted to his rhythm of going to bed early, walking slowly and breathing with difficulty.

What is more, the world became quite boring for him, now that he could no longer talk about his illness.

A young African had come to photograph my heart.

On his index finger – rather than on his ring finger, like most people – he had a silver ring with a square stone, that is, a combination of two stones: a large turquoise in the form of a tear was integrated into a black square of onyx. For the next half-hour, as I watched him work, I looked at that ring.

In order to photograph my heart, he used a hand-held scanner, and moved the cold, egg-shaped object over my breastbone, on the left side of my naked chest. On the monitor in front of him, was he focusing on the image of my heart? Or some other visual content? I don't know, I couldn't see what he was seeing. I always felt a bit dizzy whenever I heard my own heart. My hand sometimes falls unconsciously onto my chest, on the left side, just as I am falling asleep, then I become aware of my heart, and that wakes me up. And now, as that young man was recording me, I was seething with discomfort. At one moment he pressed the round scanner hard down between my ribs. This was a moment of utter bodily discomfort.

'What are you doing?'

'I'm trying to make a bit of space between your ribs, so that I get a clearer image.'

I can easily handle pain.

But this wasn't pain; this was separating the ribs right by the heart, this was far more than I was prepared to put up with. And that pressure between my ribs unleashed an uncontrollable fury in me. He had been scanning for half an hour already – had he taken any images? He said he had, but that it wasn't enough. And I told him that for me what he had already recorded was absolutely enough, pulled my pyjamas over my chest and crossed my arms over it for good measure, to prevent any further approach to my ribs.

It was as the young man, confused by my reaction, was putting away the instrument and leaving the room that Sanja stood with a decaf in a cardboard cup. She noticed my agitation and asked – what happened? I waved my hand, never mind, nothing, the examination took too long and that was why I was irritated. But then, I was put out by the expression on the young man's face. While he was packing up his apparatus, I noticed a smile of mild revolt on his face. Did he think I was a racist? That was it! I could see it in his expression. That's what he thought. He thought that I reacted the way I did not because I didn't enjoy having him forcing my ribs apart, but because I had something against the colour of his skin. I felt a need to talk to him, to put him right, but I knew that could only increase the misunderstanding.

So I didn't say anything.

Nor did he.

He left without a word.

Then Sanja appeared with a decaf in a cardboard cup. She told me some of my friends were calling and wanted to visit me in hospital.

No, no.

They wanted to assure themselves that the heart attack had happened to me, and not to them. That was human and normal, they wanted to confront the confirmation that the misfortune had passed them by.

I refused.

The third day.

I was moved out of intensive care into an ordinary hospital ward, where I shared a room with this old man. He was a Slovak by origin.

Lukas Cierny. That's what was written in blue felt tip on a little board on the wall, to the right of his bed. Nice name. Lukas Cierny. How old could he be? Eighty? Maybe more. He had Alzheimer's disease, and some chest problems, and his breathing was very restricted.

In the middle of the night he got out of bed and set off somewhere, and they brought him back from the corridor. 'Where were you going?'

'I want to get dressed and go for a walk.'

Old Cierny is much loved, there's a procession all day long of his children, grandchildren and great-grandchildren. They fill our room with laughter while they fix their father's, grandfather's or great-grandfather's pillows under his head, comb the sparse hairs on his skull and do whatever they can to please him. It is clear from the old man's vacant gaze that he doesn't know who all these people are. They turn to me as well, kindly, as though we'd always known one another and were related. The mere fact that I came from a Slavic part of the world gave them the right to that familiarity. Even though their own Slavic origin was pretty foreign to them. His daughter, when she introduced herself to me, said of Lukas: 'He's from Czechoslovakia.' She was a pure-blooded American, from Pennsylvania.

He, who remembered nothing any more, answered questions in English and then sometimes in Slovak. When he replied in Slovak, the people he was talking to didn't understand him. However, that didn't bother any of them, they weren't conversing with him in order to exchange information, but to simulate communication.

Someone had just come into the room and greeted Lukas with 'How you doin'?', to which he replied: '*Dobro*.' It was a reflex response in Slovak, a language which at this time was evidently closer to him. The person to whom the old man directed his '*dobro*' did not understand the word. The old man had been separated from his Slovak language for some seventy years. And now the word came out of him, as it were, unconsciously. But this linguistic muddle had an emotional effect on me. As though now, close to death, the old man was preparing to face death in his own language. When he pronounced his '*dobro*' it confirmed for me that I was in a foreign, distant land. Sanja was sitting by my bed, and when she heard the old man say '*dobro*', as though in our shared language, her eyes automatically filled with tears.

Later, I heard Cierny breathing with difficulty, as though he were having an asthma attack. That lasted for a while, and then he calmed down, and I no longer heard his breathing. And each time that happened, I thought he had died.

In the course of the evening, the nurses who looked after the two of us changed.

That evening there was an African Muslim girl wearing a violet silk scarf, with full make-up, including bright red lipstick, as though she was going out for the evening, to a restaurant and not a hospital ward. She was quite cheerful and sweet, young. She may have been twenty, perhaps twenty-five, but she addressed Lukas Cierny and me as though we were children.

'Where are you from?' I asked.

She laughed, and asked back: 'Where do you think?'

'Ethiopia?'

'Close.'

'Sudan.'

'Close,' she said, and waited for the guessing game to go on. But I didn't feel like going on guessing, so, disappointed with my faint-heartedness, she admitted: 'Somalia.'

She stood in front of the board – on which she was going to write her name and mine – and asked, with a felt tip in her hand: 'What's your name?'

After a brief hesitation, I replied: 'Me'med.'

From the perspective in which we found ourselves, the differences that are so fundamental to us became unimportant: whether she was from Sudan or Somalia? That mattered only to her; it left the entire continent where she now lived – indifferent. And the entire cosmos was indifferent to the differences in our identities. Seen from the perspective of death, it was a matter of total indifference which of the two of us was Slovak, and which Bosnian, Lukas and Me'med, patients stuck in the same room.

Just before midnight (she had come into our room to take blood samples), the young Somali girl asked the old Slovak: 'What's your name?'

He said nothing. She asked: 'And what year is this?'

'1939!'

That's what he said: *1939*.

What did 1939 mean to him? He must have been ten, perhaps fifteen then. That was the year before the big war. Maybe that was when he had to leave his home for good, and now, in his old age, it turned out that he had never left that year. Truly, what had happened to him in 1939? I would have liked to hear his story, but he was no longer in a state to tell it.

There's a year in my past I've never left as well.

1992.

Sometimes I'm woken by the clattering of Kalashnikovs over Sarajevo. I get up, make coffee and stay awake till morning. Through the window I look at the lights of Washington, or snow falling over the Pentagon.

During the night, Lukas Cierny got out of bed, and the young Somali put him back. 'Where were you going?'

He replied: 'To get dressed, I must go for a walk.'

He didn't actually know he was in hospital.

Then in the morning, when she was encouraging us to get out of bed, he refused, and she ordered him loudly: 'Get up! Stand up!'

'No!' said the old man.

And then – over the old Slovak who was refusing to get out of bed – she began to sing: 'Get up, stand up, stand up for your rights!' Youth is beautiful in its arrogance.

The young Somali girl, with her turquoise scarf, with her new make-up, gleamed in the morning light, bending over the Slovak at the end of his life. She was happy because she was at the end of her shift, and singing.

I was waiting very impatiently to be let out of hospital.

In fact I was afraid this wouldn't happen today. It was Friday, and that would mean I'd have to stay here over the weekend.

But the doctor appeared and asked me to walk down the corridors hooked up to all those sensors and sonars. I walked down the corridors while the doctor followed the behaviour of my heart on the monitor in front of him. I enjoyed that walk: in an hour I'd be outside, beyond the hospital walls.

When I came back into the room, the doctor checked the working of my heart once again, this time with a stethoscope and, as he didn't find any sinister sounds in my chest, in the end he gave me precise instructions about how to behave – when I got out of hospital.

And then I could go home.

I looked at him. He was Indian, he was called Rayard. And I thought: This man saved my life and we're parting like complete strangers.

I said: 'You saved my life.'

He said: 'Yes.'

And left.

After that a smiling middle-aged man arrived, with a mauve bow tie ('I'm your limo driver'), and took me in a wheelchair through the corridors to the main entrance. This was a hospital ritual. Regardless of the fact that I could walk, a man I had never seen before was pushing me in a wheelchair out of the hospital. There was something childish in that ritual move out of the world of the sick into the world of the healthy.

I parted from the stranger warmly, as though we had always known each other, and was left alone in front of the hospital. The fresh November air startled me. I'd been impatient to leave, and now that I was on the street, waiting for my taxi, I felt a mild uncertainty, and fear.

When you come back from a journey, you find things just as you left them at the moment of departure. After all the days of being away, you are now back in your own room, perhaps there's an ashtray on the desk with a cigarette butt in it, perhaps a half-finished glass of wine, or a book you were reading on the day you left, open. Everything that retains a living trace of your presence in these objects becomes an image of the time that has passed and cannot ever be replaced.

I came back from hospital and the first thing I saw from the doorway was the nice cover on the bed, the one with the floral design à la Paul Gauguin, which had come home before me. Washed, it lay over the bed, and its textile essence was unchanged – there was no trace on it of the hospital, or of my illness.

Sanja had carefully removed from all the rooms most traces I had left of my previous life, which, according to the doctors' instructions, I ought to give up. There were no ashtrays. The smell of tobacco smoke had quite disappeared from the air.

I went into the sunroom, my covered balcony, my office.

I wasn't there either.

Erased from my rooms, now I could start over.

And then, reluctantly, I went into the bathroom, where it all began. I undressed and stood in front of the mirror. I looked at the area beside my genitals. It was no longer a swelling but a bruise that was growing pale, with reddish edges, almost the colour of rust.

I shaved.

Then I stepped cautiously into the shower, listening to the behaviour of my body. The water was too hot. There was no pain in my neck, no pressure in my chest. Nothing hurt. The bathroom filled with warm steam. Water poured over me; was there anything simpler than this? A naked body with water pouring over it?

And I remembered a short film called *The Room*.

This is the story: a young man walks down the street as the light is fading, and through the open window of a room, above him, he hears the sound of a piano. And he stops. Then he sees the silhouette of the girl who was playing the piano. But the reason he stops is not only the music he heard, nor only the girl whose silhouette he saw. He does not know where that attraction comes from, he does not know the reason for his stopping, but he is aware of a strong magnetic pull emanating from that room, sensed through the open window. And years pass. He leaves that town and lives all over the world, then, as an old man, he returns. He buys an apartment, and lives out his last years in it. One day, after bathing, he leaves his room and hears the siren of an ambulance stopping in front of his building. It is night. And then he becomes conscious of everything. The room where he now finds himself is the room he had once seen, as a young man, while the sound of a piano reached him through the open window. And why had he felt such a strong attraction? The young man could not have known what the old man knew now: what he had seen then was *his* room, the one in which, when the time came, he would die.

I came out of the shower; wrapped in a towel I walked through the whole apartment. Now I'm looking out of the window, and I say: 'This is not *that* room.'

Sanja hears me. She stands behind me, leaning her head against my wet back, and asks: 'What did you say?' ■

THE MAGAZINE OF NEW WRITING

SUBSCRIPTION FORM FOR UK, EUROPE AND REST OF THE WORLD

Yes, I would like to take out a subscription to *Granta*.

GUARANTEE: If I am ever dissatisfied with my *Granta* subscription, I will simply notify you, and you will send me a complete refund or credit my credit card, as applicable, for all un-mailed issues.

YOUR DETAILS

MR / MISS / MRS / DR ....

NAME ....

ADDRESS ....

....

POSTCODE ....

EMAIL ....

☐ Please tick this box if you do not wish to receive special offers from *Granta*

☐ Please tick this box if you do not wish to receive offers from organizations selected by *Granta*

YOUR PAYMENT DETAILS

1) ☐ Pay £32.00 (saving £20) by Direct Debit
To pay by Direct Debit please complete the mandate and return to the address shown below.

2) Pay by cheque or credit/debit card. Please complete below:

1 year subscription: ☐ UK: £36.00 ☐ Europe: £42.00 ☐ Rest of World: £46.00

3 year subscription: ☐ UK: £96.00 ☐ Europe: £108.00 ☐ Rest of World: £126.00

I wish to pay by ☐ CHEQUE ☐ CREDIT/DEBIT CARD

Cheque enclosed for £________ made payable to *Granta*.

Please charge £ ________ to my: ☐ Visa ☐ Mastercard ☐ Amex ☐ Switch/Maestro

Card No. ☐☐☐☐☐☐☐☐☐☐☐☐☐☐☐☐

Valid from *(if applicable)* ☐☐☐☐ Expiry Date ☐☐☐☐ Issue No. ☐☐

Security No. ☐☐☐

SIGNATURE .... DATE ....

Instructions to your Bank or Building Society to pay by Direct Debit

BANK NAME ....

BANK ADDRESS ....

POSTCODE ....

ACCOUNT IN THE NAMES(S) OF: ....

SIGNED ....

DATE ....

DIRECT Debit

Instructions to your Bank or Building Society: Please pay Granta Publications direct debits from the account detailed on this instruction subject to the safeguards assured by the direct debit guarantee. I understand that this instruction may remain with Granta and, if so, details will be passed electronically to my bank/building society. Banks and building societies may not accept direct debit instructions from some types of account.

Bank/building society account number

☐☐☐☐☐☐☐☐

Sort Code

☐☐☐☐☐☐☐☐

Originator's Identification

9 1 3 1 3 3

Please mail this order form with payment instructions to:

Granta Publications
12 Addison Avenue
London, W11 4QR
Or call 0500 004 033
or visit GRANTA.COM

ORDINARY LIGHT

A.L. Kennedy

Which do you remember, the first time you saw an X-ray, or the first time you felt a kiss? Both? For me, it's both.

The X-ray was one of several forming part of my semi-perpetual wider education. I am the daughter of a schoolteacher and a university lecturer – education was never far away. And often I loved it. In this case, certainly I did. I can recall the stiff, mostly blue transparencies, one showing a hand. My hand was holding the secrets of another, lifting them to catch the light: bone details, flesh ghosts, the hidden construction that made for dexterity and a primate's cleverness. My own hands tended to fail the playground tests of little-girl accomplishments: catching, cat's cradle, clapping games. But now I could be sure that inside I glowed with wonders. I was some strange balance of thought and meat. I had a sense of being more transparent, permeable, increasingly at risk and yet increasingly alive.

The kiss? I had decided that kissing would eventually commence and practice would be necessary and here I was at someone's birthday party and here was a boy with lips, so why not begin? The sensations involved weren't wonderful, but did have promise: if this boy were some other boy and I were to care, then a kiss might somehow be a good thing. And I had a sense of being more transparent, permeable, increasingly at risk and yet increasingly alive.

The bewildering and lovely fact that I am both cerebral and animal pursues me. My body can let my intellect down like a drunk aunt at a party, my thinking can unleash cascades of physical unrest. My stresses produce illnesses, my illnesses produce stress. My fabric can sustain me, but will then betray me and in the end I will end – it's a truth too large to grasp. And yet it seems I have always tried to. And that's why, when I viewed sample pictures from Brad Feuerhelm's collection, I felt exhilarated, fascinated, ashamed and at home. Here were humanity's wilder beauties and our horrors, the physical record of hatreds, lusts and quiet obsessions – recurring Edwardian pictures of women standing with their backs to the photographer and showing their long, long hair. I was looking at medical curiosities, professional freaks, wounds, infections, war crimes and war criminals, victims and perpetrators and multiple opportunities to reinhabit the gaze of more and less strange, more and less emotional, observers.

Why do we look? Why do I look? Why have I always looked? Because I have. Brad's pictures explore all the refuges my mind has scrambled to in hopes of understanding my body and my nature. I've never escaped the delusion that if I know my flesh I can defend it and defend myself from it, that if I study hard enough I will unfailingly see the predator or the protector among my fellows and so be safe. Somewhere, I feel, is the secret to fox my waiting death.

I know I'm wrong, but my pursuit of body knowledge has often been, nonetheless, wonderful. My grandfather began it. He introduced me to sideshow wisdom from the strong men, the endurers, Houdini's extreme physical feats. Supernaturally strong and huge and tender, Grandpop bombarded me with medical information – he was a St John Ambulance man – and self-defence techniques – he had been a boxer, only once defeated. He saw the body in terms of vulnerabilities and strengths and wanted me to be impregnably safe. He told me, in a blushing flurry, how to avoid ungallant attentions – *Don't let them put their hand on your leg*. I still see that touch as something of a Rubicon, the point where the mind will give way to the body, and why not be better informed about hands and legs as a preparation?

My life has made all kinds of preparation. When I look at Brad's portrait of Freddie the Armless Wonder, or Jo Jo the Dog Boy, I smile and grow nostalgic because they were my childhood's companions. I thought of them as courageous and precious people. I pored over articles about Chang and Eng, the famous Siamese twins, or the perils of Spontaneous Human Combustion, or the torments that others endured in fact and fiction. I was trying to ready myself for my future. I knew it was dangerous out there and I knew I was an undisclosed freak, not least because I had to look. Some of us do. Some seek the unusual to mock, to reassure ourselves we're snugly tucked inside the bland, fat heart of the bell curve. Some of us – myself among them – assume everyone is unusual, that our frailties unite us for good and ill. Some of us succeed in never really seeing and, I suppose, believe that brings a kind of safety.

When we become complicit in making others invisible and unsayable, we help them disappear, give them a little death. Historically I am aware that one type of disappearance tends to rehearse other more permanent damages. And I'm aware that, currently, our language tiptoes round 'special needs' as if those who have them cannot even be named while we fail to protest the removal of disability benefits. I worked for ten years with people who looked and sounded and sometimes behaved in unusual ways and found their company only admirable. But for many, they were invisible, shameful. My society condemns freak shows, while watching shock TV documentaries, devouring online extremities and kinks. We look without ever risking an answering gaze. We both mock and require body modifications, impose perfections no body can meet. Brad's *cartes de visite* for human beings like Lucia Zarate – *It is difficult to describe in words this wonderful Mexican pygmy* – suddenly seem almost innocent, functional. Other pictures – *human specimen similar to monkey* – show a pseudo-scientific loathing which is truly freakish.

Some of Brad's photographs bring me to a place of enforced distress. Here are the ends of unrecorded lives. Here are the monsters with entirely human faces. The wonders and secrets and horrors of others, their truths are fugitive, even if we really look. And it's destruction that draws our attention, that speaks more loudly than normality, that wins the picture. A skull with a bullet hole faces the camera in El Salvador – *The view from the White House is far different from that at the rocky graves*. Are there some people we'll only allow to be eloquent in death?

Brad shows me hands, heads, scalps, mouths all rendered utterly alien, extinguished by malevolence or simple accident. As a species, we have such pretensions and yet we are also this: fragility and spoiled meat. And I am petty and churlish with people and yet they are also this. And I fear and condemn those of whom I disapprove and yet they are also this. And I waste so much time and yet I will come to this. And often I love those I love and kiss them with inadequate attention and yet they will come to this. A truth too large to grasp.

Of course, in the end, my strong and huge and tender grandfather died. The nurses left me to sit with his body. They thought it would help me understand. ■

ORDINARY LIGHT

From the Collection

of

Brad Feuerhelm

Douche à l'Etablissement Thermal d'Aix

G BRUN, PHOT AIX LES BAINS

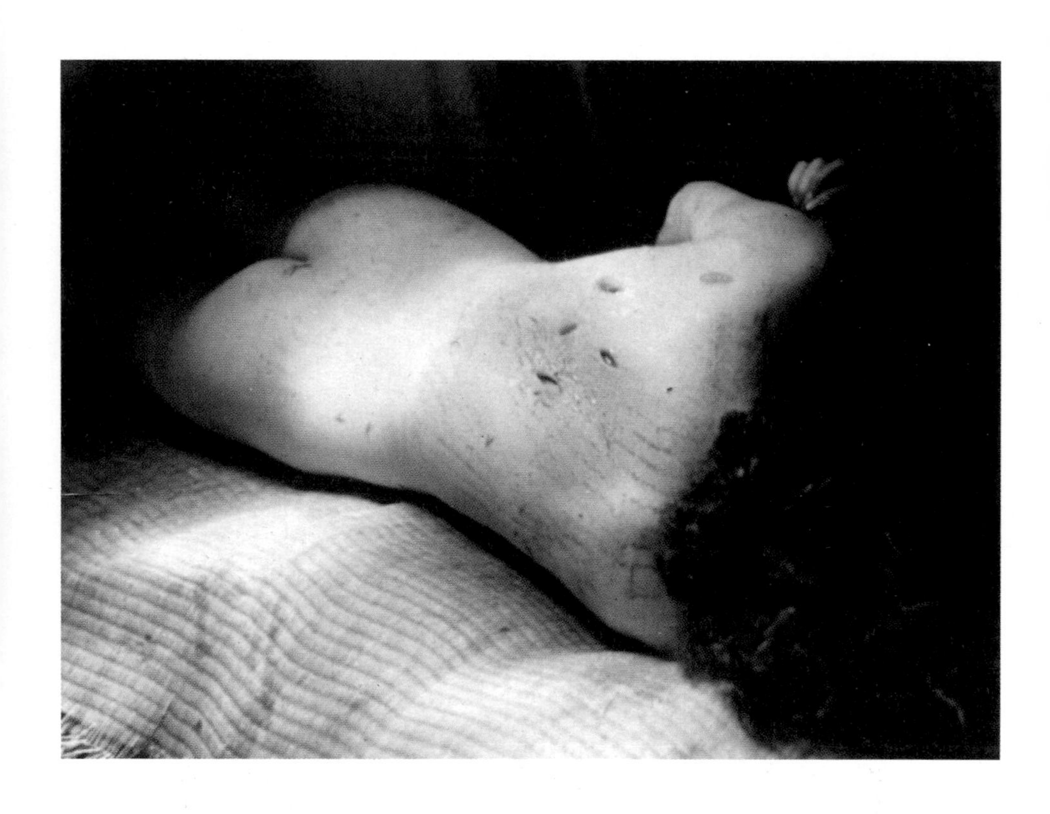

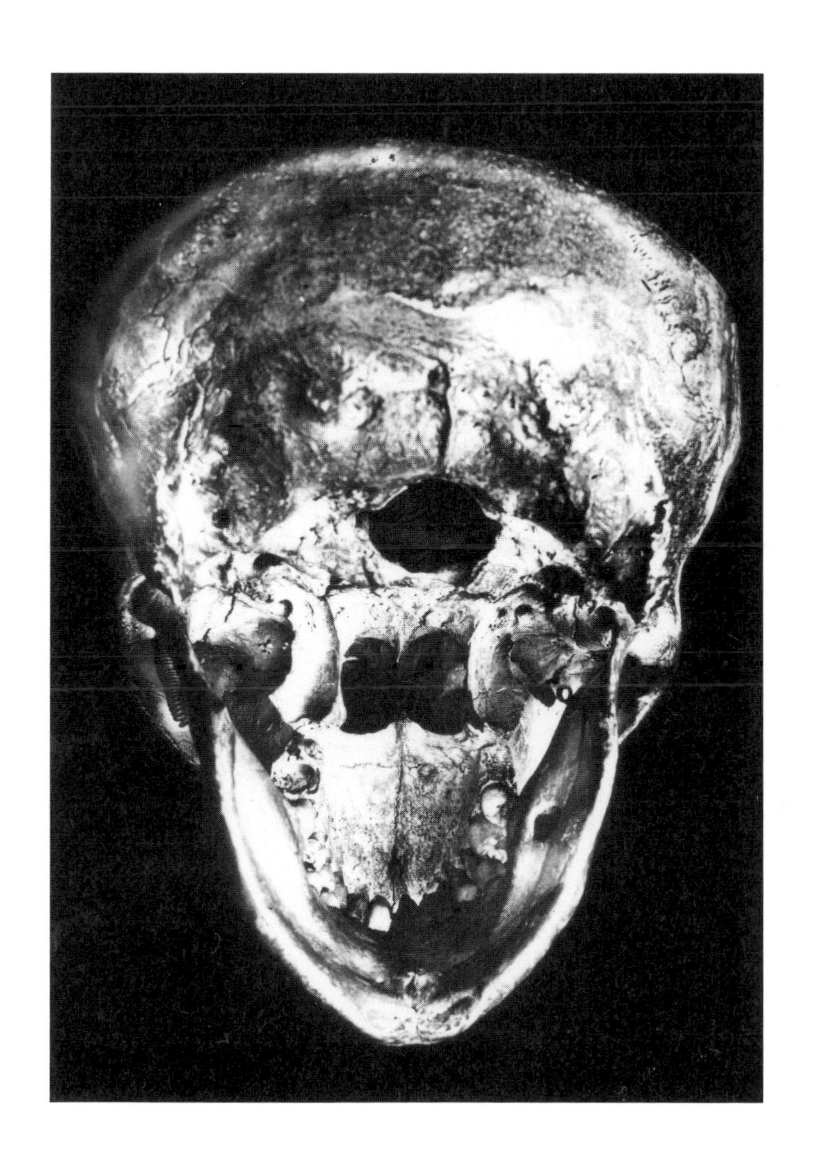

Thibault
Cor. Winooski Avenue and North Union St.
BURLINGTON, VERMONT.

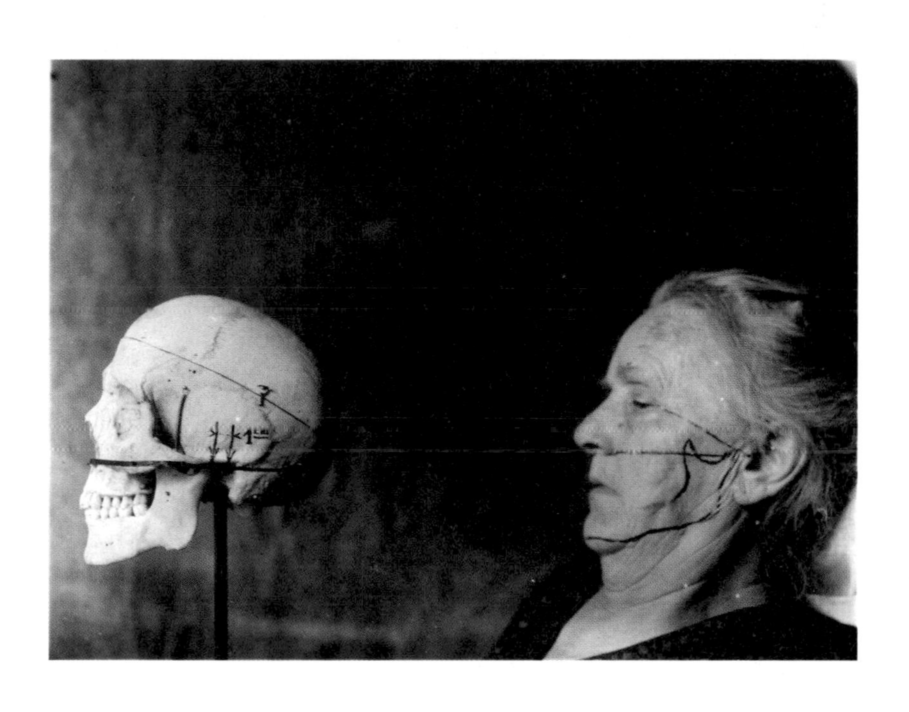

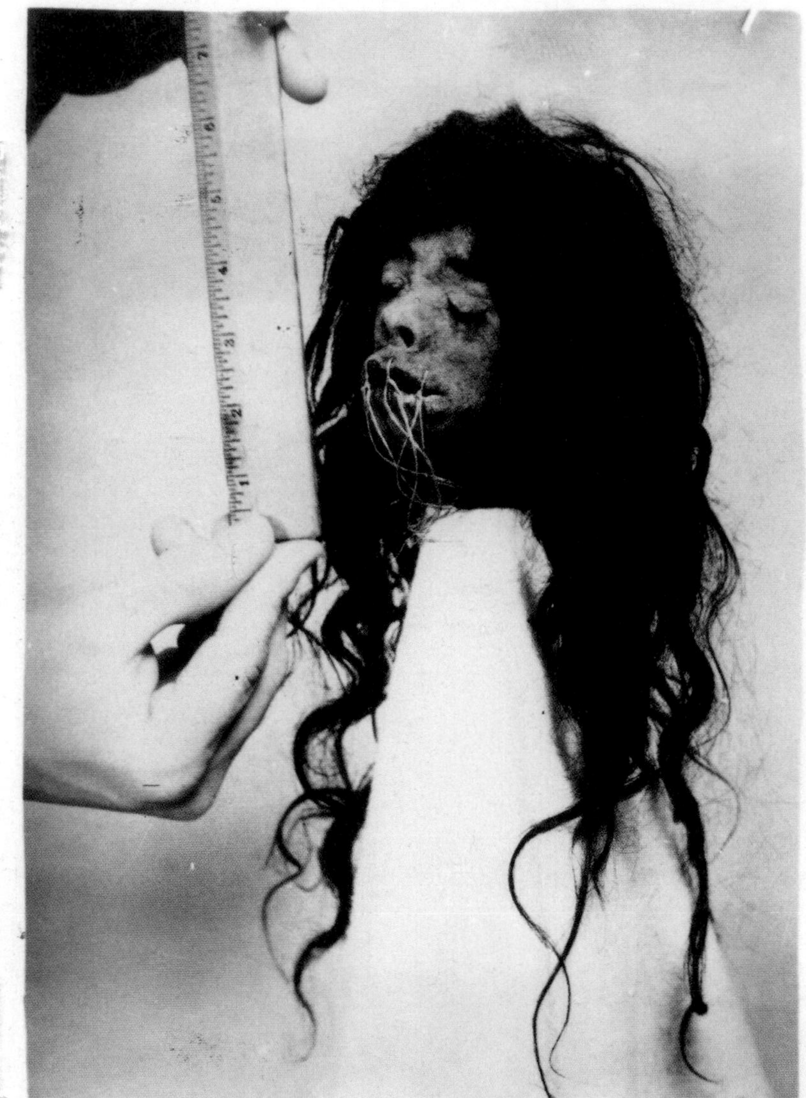

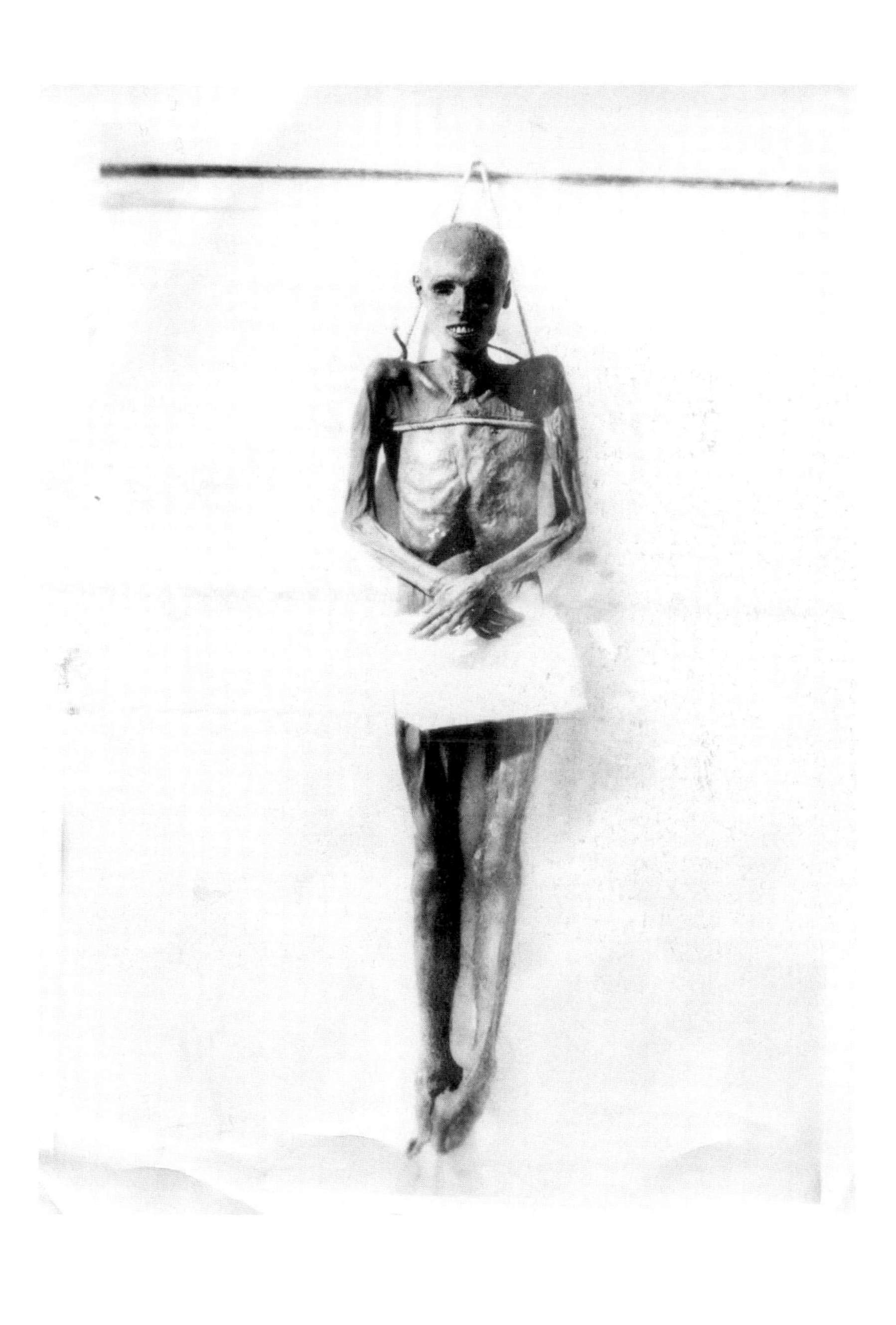

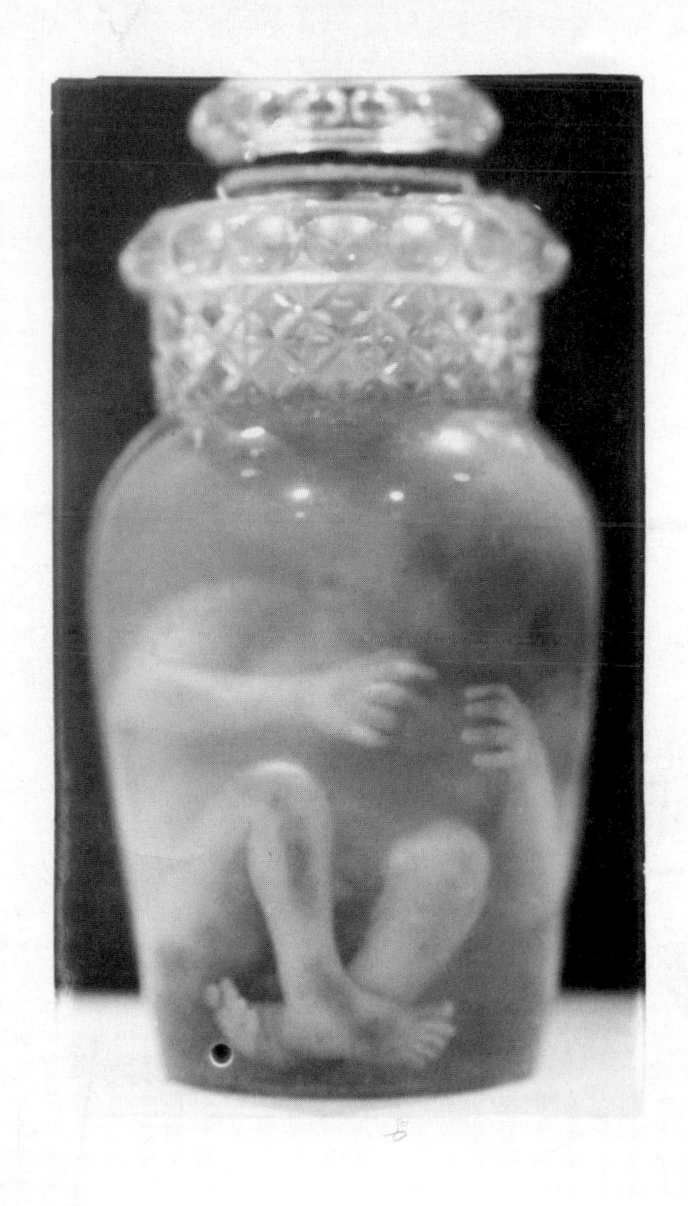

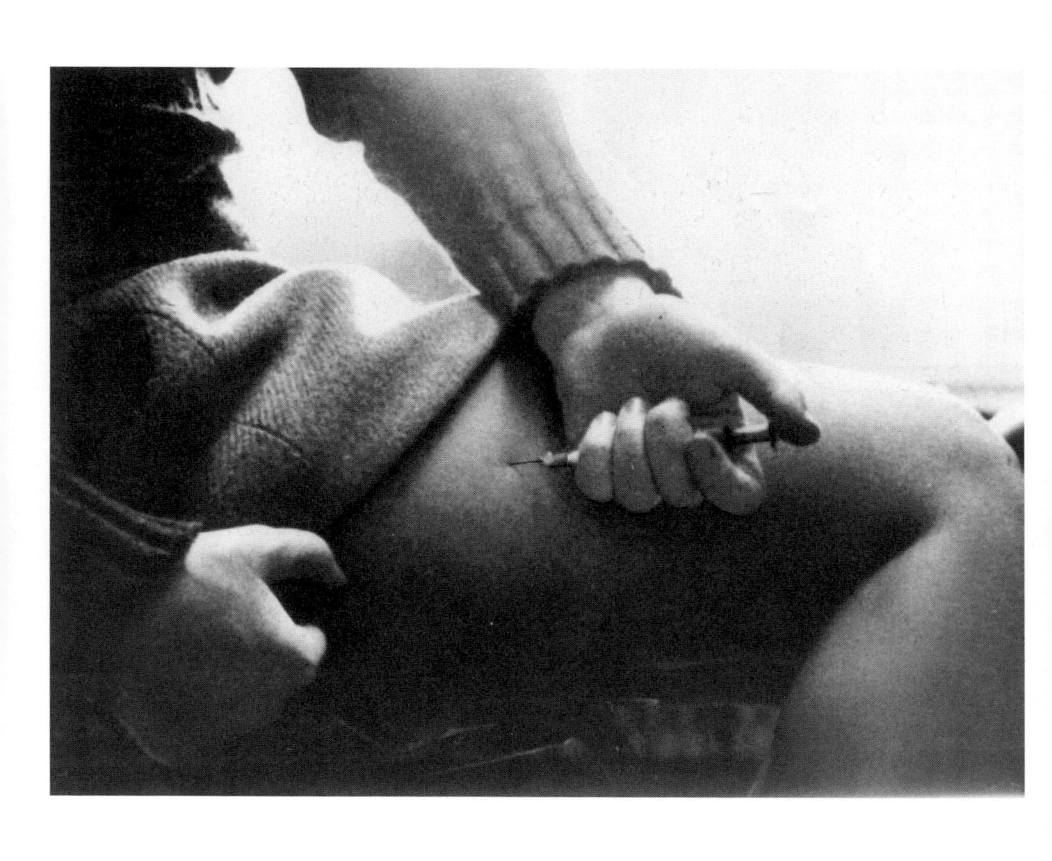

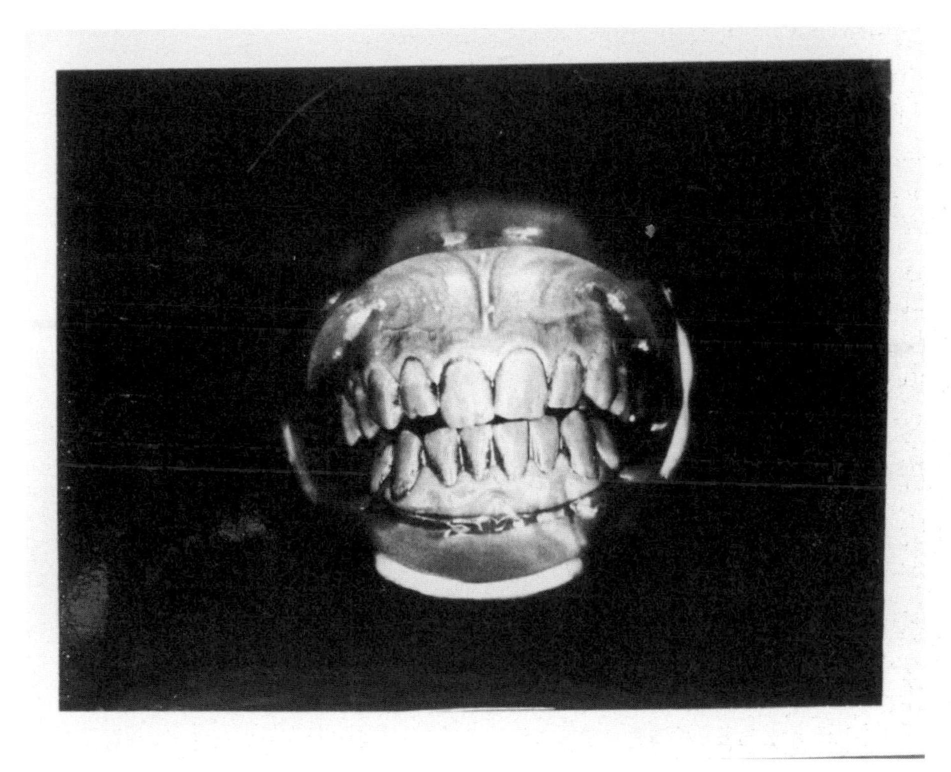

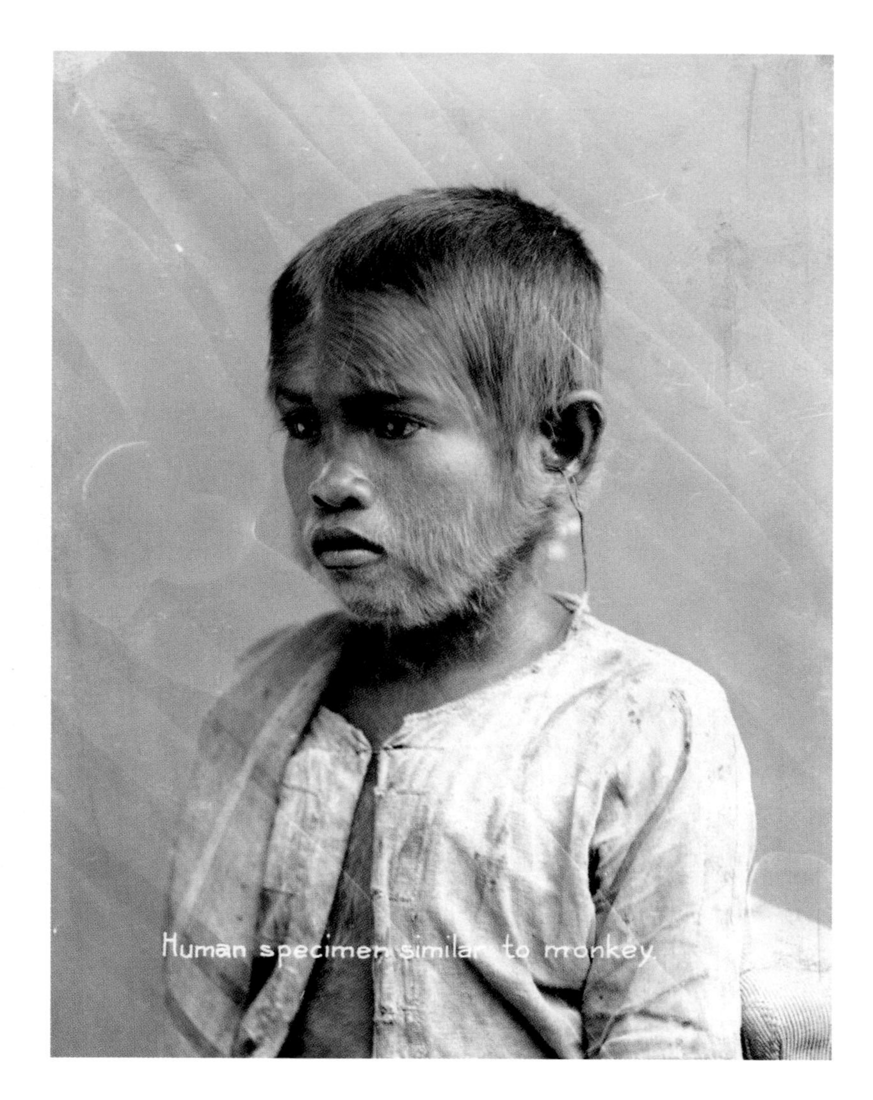
Human specimen similar to monkey.

20

MICH
RJ·97·41

R. ROBERT RICHARDSON, M. D.
81 HIGHLAND AVENUE
SALEM, MASS.

Pictures
Taken while
I was a clerk
at Concord State Hosp
Summer '41

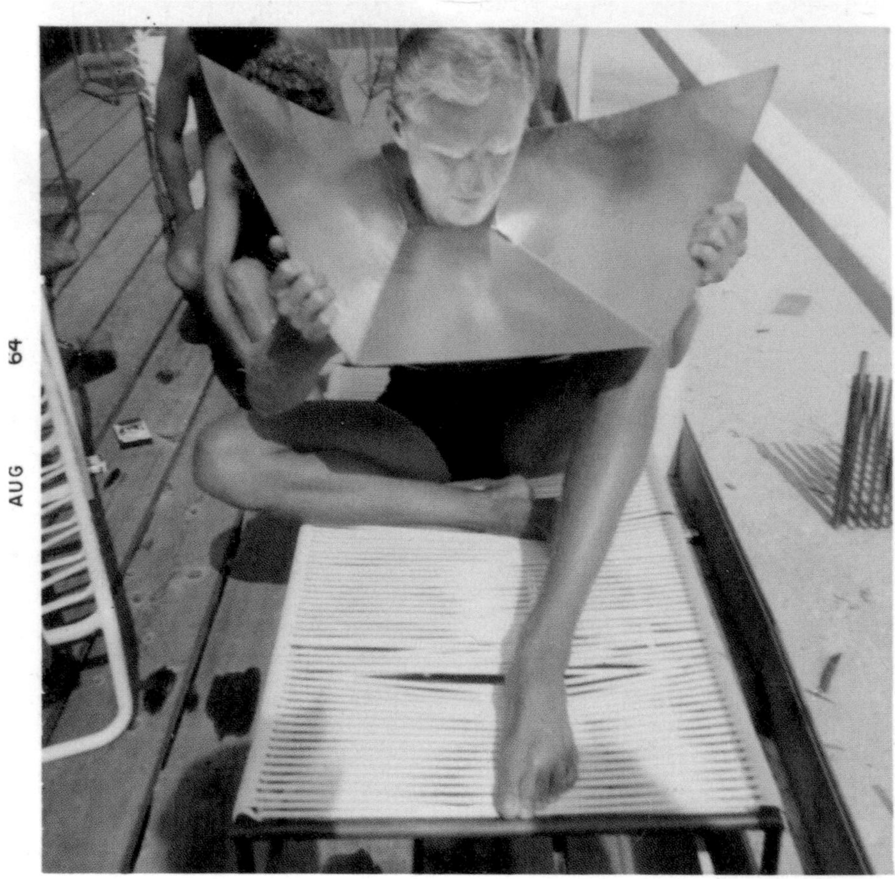

AUG 64

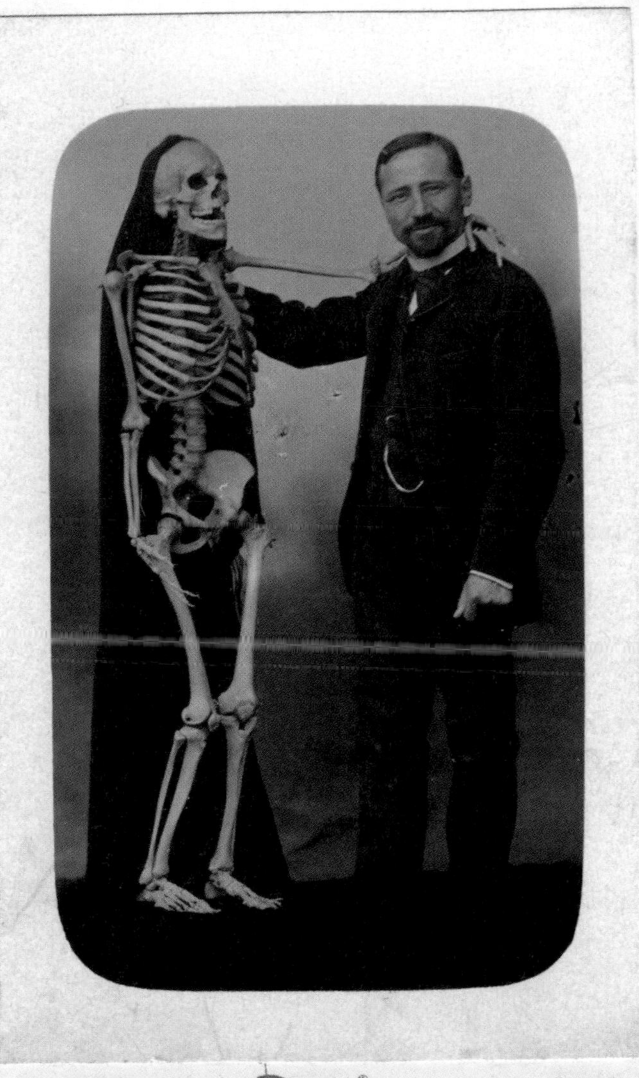

J. Odin

#28
Dogs actually eating a Corpse.

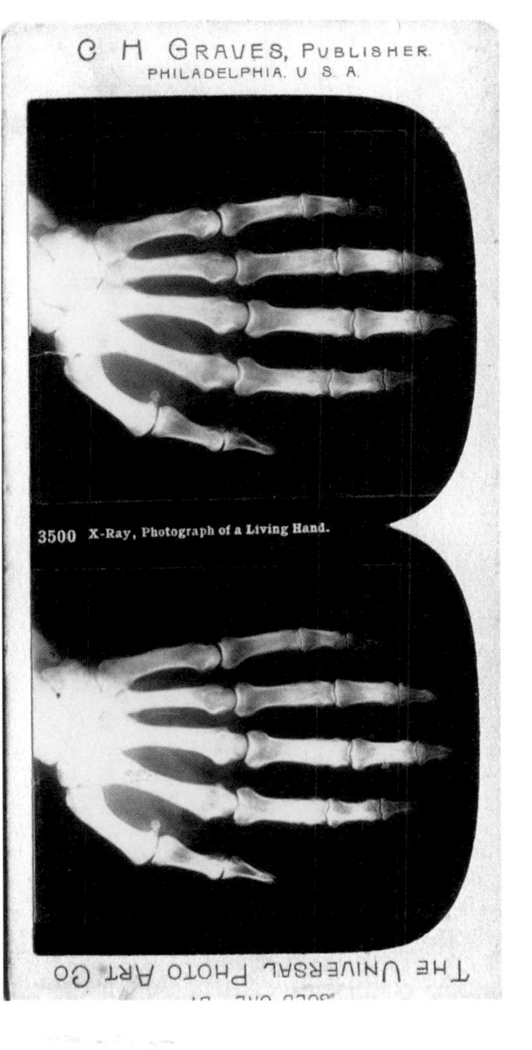
C H GRAVES, PUBLISHER.
PHILADELPHIA. U S. A.
3500 X-Ray, Photograph of a Living Hand.
THE UNIVERSAL PHOTO ART CO

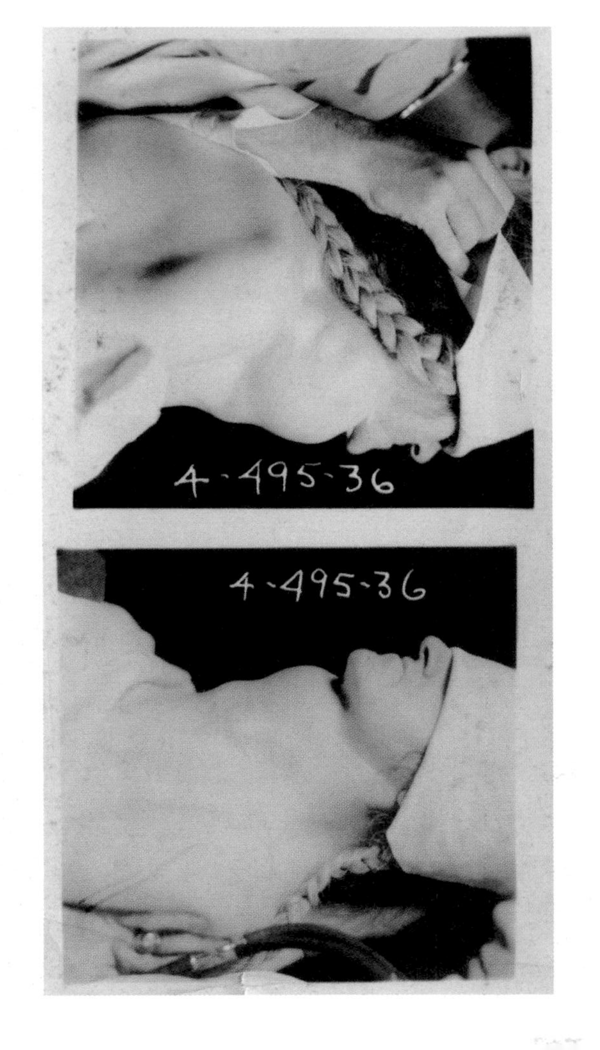
4-495-36
4-495-36

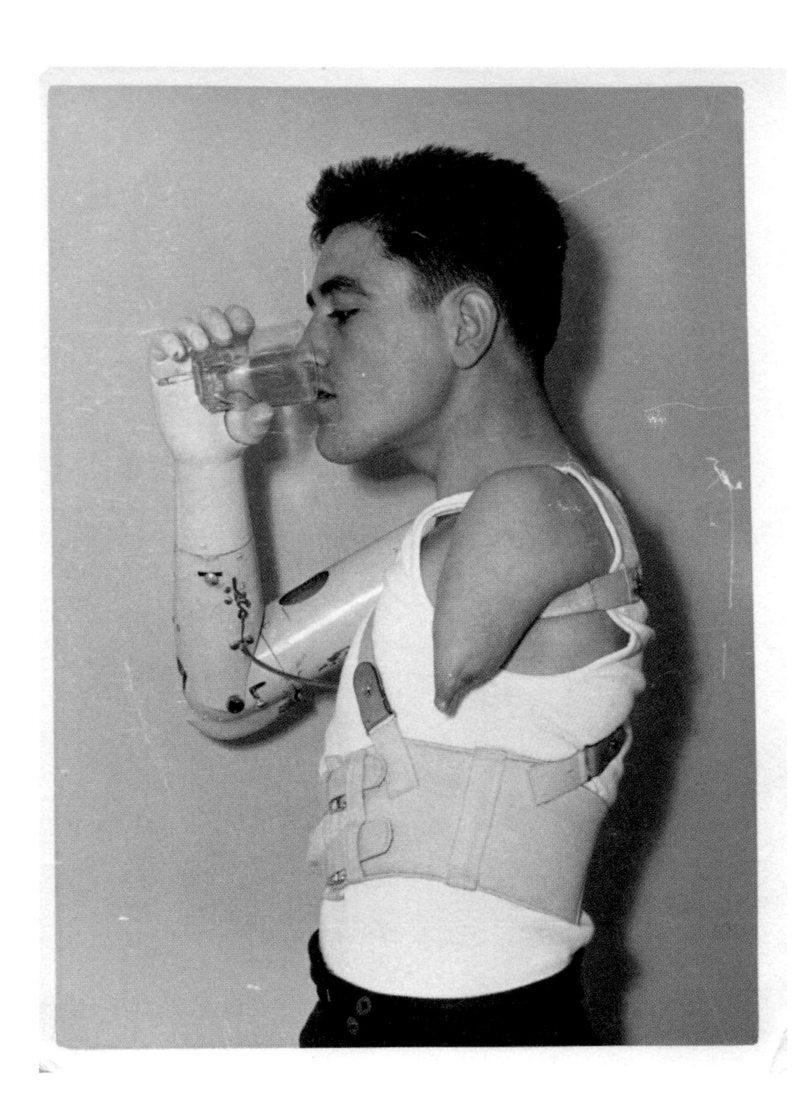

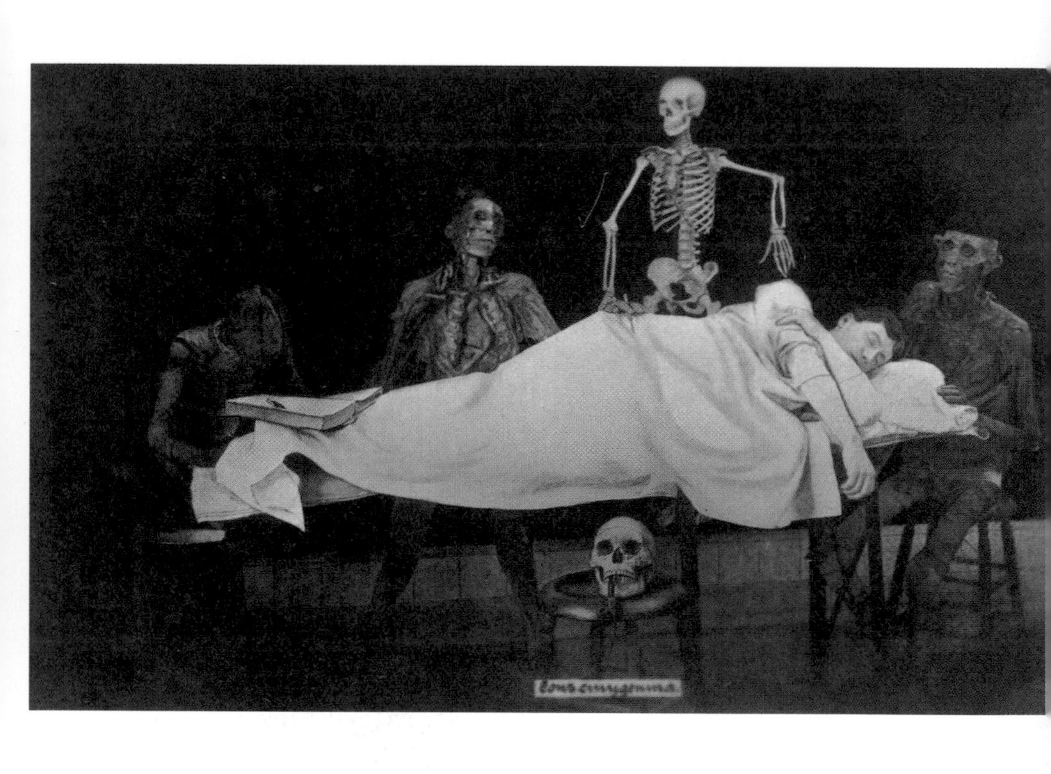

POEM | KAY RYAN

Nature Study: Spots

Like something
that might also
happen in the head,
they are strange
rings that flatten
and spread chalky
grey vaccination
spots on bays,
creating an exact
but dimensionless
perimeter against
the deep knap of
ferns and mosses
that coat the trunk.
All that dense life:
kept out as though
these patches were
moon or had been
bombed. Reminding us
again that live things
can be flat. And flat
can stop green things
like that.

The Royal Society of Literature
THE ROYAL SOCIETY OF LITERATURE
G·IV·R

THE PERFECT CODE

Terrence Holt

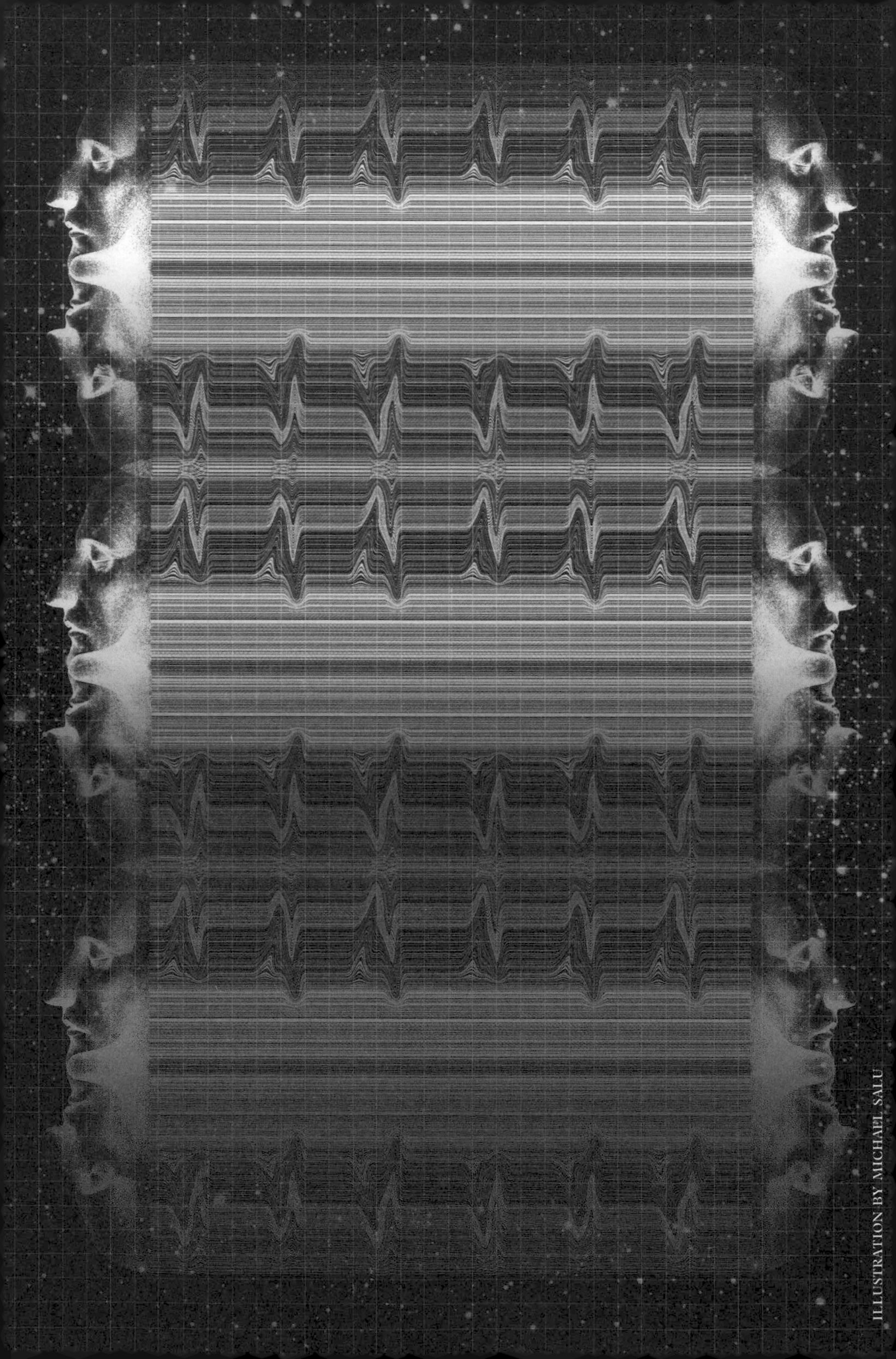
ILLUSTRATION BY MICHAEL SALU

A faint click opens the air. A disembodied voice calls out: 'Adult Code 100, Adult Code 100, 5 East. Adult Code 100, 5 East.' Or it might be 'Code Blue, Code Blue 3C, Code Blue 3C.' From place to place the wording varies, but the message is always the same: somewhere in the hospital, someone is dying.

Hearts stop. Vital signs droop. Whatever the nature of the emergency, the response is the same: from all over the hospital the code team comes running, and the attempt at resuscitation begins.

I'm not sure, still, just what I learned running to so many codes, but the experience haunts me, long after the fact. As if somewhere in the tangle of tubes and wires, knotted sheets, Betadyne and blood, I lost track of something important. Listen.

In the hospital where I work, codes go something like this. A nurse finds a patient slumped over in bed. The nurse calls her name. No answer. The nurse shakes the inert body. No answer. Harder. Still no answer. The nurse steps to the door and calls, in tones that rise at each syllable, 'I need some help here.' The rest of the available nurses on the floor converge. Within a minute, every bystander within hearing is gathered at the door.

In the basement of the hospital, an operator listens intently to her headset. She flips a switch, and a faint click opens the hospital to the microphone on her console. 'Adult Code 100, 6 South. Adult Code 100, 6 South.' The message goes out on the hospital PA system, her disembodied voice filling the hallways. It also goes out to a system of antique voice pagers, from which the operator's measured words emerge as inarticulate squealing. The pagers are largely backup, in case some member of the team is, say, in the bathroom, or otherwise out of reach of the PA system.

The team consists of eight or nine people: respiratory techs, anaesthesiologists, pharmacists, and the residents on call for the Cardiac ICU. On hearing the summons, the residents drop whatever they are doing and sprint. In their voluminous white coats, from whose pockets fall stethoscopes, penlights, reflex hammers, EKG calipers, tuning forks, ballpoint pens (these clatter across the floors to be scooped up by the medical students who follow behind), the medical team's passing is a curious combination of high drama and burlesque.

The team arrives on a scene of Bedlam. The room is so crowded with nurses, CNAs, janitors and miscellaneous onlookers that it can be physically impossible to enter. Shouldering your way through the mob at the door, you are stopped by a crowd around the bed; the crash cart, a rolling red metal Sears Roebuck tool chest, is also in the way, its open drawers a menace to knees and elbows. There are wires draped from the crash cart and tubing everywhere.

At the centre of all this lies the patient, the only one in the room who isn't shouting. The patient doesn't move at all. This time it is an elderly woman, frail to the point of wasting; her ribs arch above her hollow belly. Her eyes are half open, her jaw is slack, pink tongue protruding slightly. Her gown and the bedding are tangled in a mass at the foot of the bed; at a glance you take in the old mastectomy scar, the scaphoid abdomen, the grey tuft between her legs. At the head of the bed, a nurse is pressing a mask over the patient's face, squeezing oxygen through a large bag; the woman's cheeks puff out with each squeeze, which isn't right. Another nurse is compressing the chest, not hard enough. You shoulder her aside and press two fingers under the angle of the jaw. Nothing. A quick listen at her chest: only the hubbub in the room, dulled by silent flesh. Pile the heels of both hands over her breastbone and start to push: the bed rolls away. Falling half onto the patient, you holler above the commotion, 'Somebody please lock the bed.' Alternate this with 'Does anyone have the chart?'

A nurse near the door hoists a thick brown binder, passing it over the heads jamming the room. 'Code status,' you bawl out. 'Full code,' the nurse bawls back. You reposition your hands and push down on her breastbone. 'Why's she here?' There is a palpable crunch as her ribs separate from her sternum. 'Metastatic breast cancer,' the nurse calls, flipping pages in the chart. 'Admitted for pain control.' You lighten up the pressure and continue to push, rhythmically, fast. You look around, trying to pick out from the mass of excited bystanders the people who belong. The noise is immense. On the opposite side of the bed you see one of the respiratory techs has arrived. 'Airway,' you shout, and the tech nods: she has already seen the puffing cheeks. She takes the mask and bag from the nurse and adjusts the patient's neck. The patient's chest starts to rise and fall beneath your hands.

'What's she getting for pain?'

'Morphine PCA.'

'What rate?'

The question sets off a flurry of activity among some nurses, one of whom stoops to examine the IV pump at the patient's bedside. 'Two per hour, one q fifteen on the lockout.'

'Narcan,' you order.

By this time, the pharmacist has arrived, which is fortunate because you can't remember the dose of opiate blocker. You doubt this is overdose here, but it's the first thing to try. Out of the corner of your eye you see the pharmacist load a clear ampoule into a syringe and pass it to a nurse.

Meanwhile on your left, the other resident and the intern are plunging large needles into both groins, probing for the femoral vein. The intern strikes blood first, removes the syringe, throws it onto the sheets. 'Send that off for labs,' you shout. Blood dribbles from the needle's hub as the intern threads a long, coiled wire through it into the vein. The other resident stops jabbing and watches the intern's progress. With a free hand she feels for the femoral pulse, but the bed is bouncing. You stop compressing. The resident focuses, shakes her head. Start compressing again.

A nurse reaches around you on the right, trying to fit a pair of metallic adhesive pads onto the patient's chest. You shake your head. 'Paddles,' you shout. 'Get me the paddles.' Then, into the general roar, 'Somebody take that syringe and send it off for labs.' A hand grabs the syringe and whisks it off. 'You!' you shout at the med student, who is hanging by the resident's elbow. 'Get a gas!' The resident throws a package from the crash cart, then steps back to give the student access to the patient's groin. The student fits the needle to the blood-gas syringe, feels for the pulse your compressions are making in the groin and stabs it home: blood, dark purple, fills the barrel. The student looks worried; he may have missed the artery.

The nurse at your elbow is still there, holding the defibrillator paddles. She stands as though she has been holding these out to you for some time. Clap the paddles on the patient's chest. Over your shoulder on the tiny screen of the defibrillator a wavy line of green light scrawls horizontally onward. You look back at the other resident. 'Anything?' You both say at once, and both of you shake heads. The intern has finished with the femoral catheter. He holds up one of the access ports. 'Amp of epi,' you say, but there's no response. Louder: 'I need an amp of epi.' Finally someone shoves a big blunt-nosed syringe into your hand. Without stopping to verify that it's what you asked for, you lean over and fit it to the port and push the plunger. Another look at the screen. Still nothing. 'Atropine,' you call out, and this time a nurse has it ready. 'Push it,' you say, and she does. Stop compressions, check the screen.

Suddenly the wavery tracing leaps into life, a jagged irregular line, teeth of a painful saw. 'V fib,' the other resident calls out, annoying you for a moment. You clamp the paddles down on the patient's ribs. 'Everyone clear?' Everyone has moved back two feet from the bed. You check your own legs, arch your back. 'Clear?' You push the button. The patient spasms, then lies limp again. The pattern on the screen is unchanged. The other resident shakes her head. You call over your shoulder, 'Three hundred,' and shock again. The body twitches again. An unpleasant smell rises from the bed.

The pattern on the screen subsides, back to the long lazy wave. Still no pulse. You start compressing again. 'Epi,' you call out. 'Atropine.' There is another flutter of activity on the screen, but before you can shock, it goes flat again, almost flat, perhaps there is a suggestion of a ragged rhythm there, fine sawteeth. 'Clear,' you call again, and everybody draws back. 'Three sixty,' you remember to say over your shoulder, and when the answering call comes back you shock again, knowing this is futile. But the patient is dead and there is no harm in trying. As the body slumps again, there is a palpable slackening of the noise level in the room, and even though you go on another ten minutes, pushing on the chest until your shoulders are burning and your breath is short, and a total of ten milligrams of epinephrine has gone in, there is nothing on the monitor that looks remotely shockable.

Finally, you straighten up and find the clock on the wall. 'I'm calling it,' you say. Against the wall, a nurse with a clipboard makes a note. 'Time?' she says. You tell her.

There is more. Picking up, writing notes, a phone call or two. There is a family member in the hallway, sitting stricken on a bench beside a nurse or volunteer holding a hand. You need to speak to her, but before you do you have to find out the patient's name. And then you go back to whatever you were doing before the code went out over the PA.

There is a great deal of mess in hospital medicine, literal and figurative, and the code bunches it all into a dense mass that on some days seems to represent everything wrong with the world. The haste, the turmoil, the anonymity, the smell, the futility: all of it brought to bear on a single body, as if to point to a moral that I would understand better if only I had time to stop and contemplate it. Which I don't. Not today. We're admitting and there are three patients, two on the floor and one down in the ER, waiting to be seen. There is no time to read the fine print on anything, least of all the mortal contract just executed on the anonymous woman lying back in the room.

I can barely make out the large block letters at the top: our patients die. And very often they do so in the middle of a scene with all the dignity of a cafeteria food fight. We can't cure everybody, but I think most of us treasure as a small consolation that at least we can afford people some kind of dignity at the end, something quiet and solemn in which whatever meaning resides in all of this may be – if we watch and listen carefully – perceptible.

Which may be why one particular code persists in my memory, long after the event.

John Mongay was the name I got from the medicine admitting officer. I wasn't sure what to make of the MAO's story, but I knew I didn't like it.

The story was a 72-year-old guy with a broken neck. He had apparently fallen in his driveway while picking up his newspaper that morning, cracking his first and second vertebrae. I had a vague memory from medical school that this wasn't a good thing – the expression 'hangman's fracture' kept bobbing up from the well of facts I do not use – but I had a much more distinct impression that this was not a case for cardiology.

'And ortho isn't taking him because?' I said wearily.

'Because he's got internal organs, dude.'

I sighed. 'So why me?'

'Because they got an EKG.'

The MAO was clearly enjoying himself. I remembered he had recently been accepted to a cardiology fellowship. I braced myself for the punchline.

'And?'

'And there's ectopy on it. *Ectopy*.' He then made a noise intended to suggest a ghost haunting something.

Ectopy, meaning literally 'out of place', refers to a heartbeat generated anywhere in the heart but the little knob in the upper right-hand corner where heartbeats are supposed to start. Such beats appear with an unusual shape and timing on the EKG. They can be caused by any number of things, from too much caffeine to fatigue to an impending heart attack, but in the absence of other warning signs, ectopy is not something we generally get excited about. And it sounded to me as though a man with a broken neck had enough reasons for ectopy without sending him to the Cardiology service.

'So?' I said.

'So he's also got a history. Angioplasty about ten years ago, no definite history of MI. You can't really read his EKG because he's got a left bundle, no old strips so I don't know if it's new.'

We were down to business.

'So I rule him out.'

'You rule him out. Ortho says they'll follow with you.'

'Lovely. And once I rule him out?'

'Ortho says they'll follow with you.'

I said something unpleasant. The MAO understood. 'Sucks, I know, but there you are.'

And there I was, down in the ER on a Sunday afternoon, turning over the stack of papers that John Mongay had generated over his six hours in the ED. There was a sheaf of EKGs covered with bizarre ectopic beats, through which occasionally emerged a stretch of normal sinus rhythm, enough to see that there was, indeed, a left bundle branch block, and not much else. The heart has several bundles, cables in its internal wiring. When some disease process disrupts a bundle, the result is an EKG too distorted to answer the question we usually ask it: Is this patient having a heart attack? Of course, the bundle itself is not a reassuring sign and, if new, it merits an investigation, but plenty of people in their seventies have them and it's pretty much a so what. But the ectopy on today's strips was impressive – if you didn't know what you were looking at you might think he was suffering some catastrophic event. I read between the lines of the consult note the orthopaedic surgeons had left, and it was clear they regarded John Mongay as a time bomb and didn't want him on their service.

Which I couldn't help noting was exactly how I felt about having a patient with a broken neck on my service. But I didn't get to make decisions like that. Instead I wadded the stack of papers back into their cubby and took a brief glance through the curtains of Bay 12. From my somewhat distorted perspective, most of what I saw of the patient was his feet, which were large, bare and protruding from the lower end of his ER blankets in a way that suggested he would be tall if I could stand him up. At his side sat a small, iron-haired woman who at that moment was speaking to him, leaning in close. She wore a faint, affectionate smile on a face that looked otherwise tired. I watched her for a moment, her profile held precisely perpendicular to my line of sight as though posed. For a moment her face took on an almost luminous clarity, a study in patience, in care – and then it wavered, receding into a small, tired woman with grey hair beside a gurney in Bay 12. The patient's face was obscured by the pink plastic horse collar that immobilized his neck. I watched the woman for a minute. Her expression, the calm progress of their conversation, suggested that nothing too drastic was going on. I took a walk to the radiology reading room to get a look at the neck films.

There were many of these, too. They showed the vulture neck silhouette all C-spine films share. There were several unusual views, including one that I decided must have been shot straight down the patient's open mouth: it showed, framed by teeth palisaded with spiky metal, the pale ring of the first vertebra, the massive bone called the atlas, and clear (even to me) on both sides of it were two jagged dark lines angling in on the empty centre where the spinal cord had failed to register on film. The break in the second vertebra was harder to make out, but I took the surgeons at their word: *C1/2 fx: cont immob pending halo. Will follow.*

I was not in the best of moods as I made my way back to the ER, grabbed a clipboard and parted the curtains to Bay 12. Still, I managed an adequate smile as I introduced myself. 'John Mongay?' I said tentatively.

The woman at his shoulder blinked up at me, wearing that same weary smile, brushing a lock of hair from her face.

'It's "Mon-zhay",' she said, with an odd combination of self-deprecation and something else – perhaps it was warmth? – that made me like her. 'It's French,' she explained. She welcomed me into Bay 12, which I had been inside more times than I cared to count, with a curious air of apology, as if concerned about the quality of her housekeeping. I was charmed. This was still relatively early in the day and I was capable of being charmed. I shook myself a little, and straightened my back (her posture was perfect).

Her husband made a less distinct impression. The cervical stabilization collar has a dampening effect on most people, as would the eight milligrams of morphine he'd absorbed over the past six hours, so it was a bleary and not very articulate history I got from him. His wife filled in the relevant bits. No prior MI. Occasional chest pain, hard to pin down. Otherwise a generally healthy, alert and active man. On the one really critical point – what had caused the fall – Mr Mongay insisted on giving account. He had *not* fainted. He had not been dizzy or breathless or experienced palpitations or anything of that sort. He had tripped. He had caught his toes on the uneven edge left by the damned contractor who'd resurfaced the driveway two years previously, and gone down like a stupid ox. As he said the last he shook his head vehemently within the confines of his collar, and I caught my breath: you're not supposed to do that with a broken neck.

Even so I was partially reassured. The history didn't suggest a cardiac cause to his fall, and he denied any of the other symptoms that go along with impending doom. The physical exam was similarly reassuring, although hampered by the cervical collar and my dread of doing anything that might disturb his neck. He was a tall, bony man, with a nasty-looking cut across the scalp above his right eye and dried blood crusted in his bushy eyebrows. The cut had been sutured already, and the blood made it look much worse than it was. Aside from the cut and a large bruise on his right ribs (none broken), he seemed fine. Except for the neck, of course. I stayed another few minutes, making idle chat with the wife, who promised me that her son and one of her three daughters would be coming back soon, and then excused myself to write my orders.

He ruled out with the 4 a.m. blood draw the next morning, which I announced on rounds a few hours later with less pleasure than I would have ordinarily. I knew what was coming.

'So now what?' the attending asked.

'I guess I call ortho.'

Everybody – from attending to fellow to the other resident on the team and the intern, even the two medical students – started to smile.

'Well, I can call them, can't I?'

'Go ahead,' the attending said.

I made the call, and after three or four hours the ortho resident returned the page. I knew by that time that I was already defeated, but I went ahead and asked the obligatory question, and received the inevitable answer (the ortho resident having anticipated as well) that the ortho attending did not feel comfortable taking the case, '. . . and besides, it's not that bad a break. We'll follow.'

'How long?' I asked.

'What do you mean?'

'How long does he need to be in the hospital?'

Puzzled. 'When will you be done with him?'

'We've been done since eight this morning.'

'You mean you'd send him home?'

'Except for the neck thing, yeah.'

'Oh.' This he hadn't anticipated.

'So what does he need from you?'

'He needs a halo.'

A halo is one of those excruciating-looking devices you may have seen somebody wearing: a ring of shiny metal that encircles the head (hence the name), supported by a cage that rests on a harness braced on the shoulders. Four large bolts run through the halo and into the patient's skull, gripping the head rigidly in place like a Christmas tree in its stand. A little crust of blood where the bolts penetrate the skin completes the picture. They look terrible, but patients tell me that after the first day or so they don't really hurt. Getting one put on, however: that hurts.

'So when does he get it?' I asked. Again, I knew the answer. It was already past noon. I was pretty sure it was Monday.

'Well,' the ortho resident replied, 'it's already past noon.'

'And you're in surgery.'

'Yeah.'

'And tomorrow?'

'Clinic. All day clinic.'

I didn't say anything. I waited a long time, biting my tongue.

'I guess we could do it tonight,' he said.

'That'd be nice.'

'Unless there's an emergency, of course.'

'Of course.'

And of course there was. And clinic ran overtime the next day, or so I was told. Their notes on the chart (they came by each morning at 5.45) ran to five scribbled lines, ending each time with 'Plan halo. Will follow,' and a signature and pager number I couldn't quite decipher. This left me holding the bag. Not only had I one more patient crowding my census, one more patient to see in the morning, round on and write notes about (this during the month our team set the record for admissions to cardiology), but I also had the unpleasant responsibility of walking into Mr Mongay's room on Tuesday and Wednesday morning to find him unhaloed, and making apologies for it.

It would have been unpleasant, at least, but for Mrs Mongay and her children. There were four in all. The son, John Jr, was a very pleasant fellow in his late thirties, intelligent, well educated, unusually sophisticated about medical matters. The three daughters were hard to tell apart – I never did learn their names – but they accepted my apologies with a sympathetic understanding. Like their mother, with their quiet grace and gentle good humour they put me in mind of faces I'd seen in old oil paintings, glowing against a warm chiaroscuro. All of which only made the situation even more intolerable, driving me to want to *do* something for them – and the only thing I had to offer lay in the gift of the inaccessible ortho resident.

Wednesday I was on call again and had pledged myself, in the brief moments between admissions, to track down the ortho team and make them come up and put that halo on. Unfortunately, this was the day we admitted fifteen patients, as the failure clinic opened its floodgates and the Cath Lab pumped out case after case. The sheer volume of histories to take, physicals to perform, notes and orders to compose was overwhelming. The phone call – with its necessary sequel of waiting for the paged resident to call back – never happened.

Sometime in the late afternoon, however, I looked up from the counter where I had been leaning, trying to absorb the salient features of yet another failure patient's complex history, and saw through the open door of Mr Mongay's room a strange tableau: two tall men in green scrubs wielding socket wrenches around the patient's head, a tangle of chrome, and the patient's hands quivering in the air, fingers spread as if calling on the seas to part. Sometime later I looked up again and the green scrubs were gone. Mr Mongay lay propped up in his bed, his head in a halo. From the side, his nose was a hawk's beak, the rest of his face sunk in drugged sleep, but his mouth still snarled as if it remembered recent pain. He looked like a strange, sad bird in a very small cage.

Still later – time on that service being marked by missed meals and sleep, I can say only that I was hungry, but not yet punchy – a nurse stopped me.

'Fourteen,' she said.

She meant Mr Mongay. 'How's he doing?' I was harbouring some vague hope that he was awake and asking to go home.

'He's complaining of chest pain. Ten out of ten.'

'Crap,' I said. The nurse looked at me. 'Get an EKG.'

My vague hope vanished entirely ten minutes later as I watched the red graph paper emerge from the side of the box. The squiggle on it looked better than the initial set from the ER, but that was only because the ectopy was gone. What was there instead – Mr Mongay's souvenir of the activities of the afternoon – were T-wave inversions marching across his precordium. This was not good. T-wave inversions generally signify heart muscle that isn't getting oxygen. What I was seeing here suggested that his LAD – a major artery supplying blood to the heart's strongest muscle – was about to choke off. I looked up at the nurse. She had been reading the strip as well, upside down, as cardiology nurses can.

'You gonna move him?' she asked.

'Yeah.'

'Write me some orders.'

'I'll write you orders. Just get him to the Unit. Quickly,' I added, with a backward glance through the door of 14.

I didn't give Mongay much thought the rest of the evening, beyond getting him scheduled as an add-on for the Cath Lab the next day. Around two in the morning the three of us – my partner Sasha, the intern Jeff and I – were gathered at one end of the long counter, pushing stacks of paper around and trying to count up the score. We were on admission twelve for the day, we decided, but couldn't remember who was up next. I was digging in my pockets for a coin to flip when my pager went off. I swore as I tugged it from my belt, expecting to find yet again the number for the ER. I found instead the number for the CCU, followed by '911'. At that moment the overhead paging system called a code in the CCU. The three of us ran.

It was perhaps thirty yards to the CCU, but by the time we got there three of the six nurses on shift were in Mongay's room, one at the head squeezing oxygen through a bag-valve mask, another compressing his chest, a third readying the crash cart. I had a moment's awareness that something was unusual – the whole thing looked too emptily staged, some kind of diorama in the Museum of Human Misery, but the scene only appeared that way for an instant and then we were in it and perspective fell apart in a surge of activity.

Sasha and I had never made any formal arrangement about who did what in a code. I was the first one on the far side of the bed and started feeling the groin for a pulse. It was faint, driven solely by the nurse's compressions, but clear enough. I grabbed a finder syringe from the tray a nurse held out to me and plunged it in. Nothing. Pull back, change angle, feel for the pulse again and drive. The needle ground against bone. On this pass I saw the flash in the syringe, pulled back to confirm, then flung the syringe aside and put a thumb over the hub of the needle while reaching for the wire. The nurse had it out already, handle turned toward me. It threaded the vein without resistance.

I had the catheter in place a minute or two later, met at each step in the process by the right item held out at the right time. No one spoke a word.

On the other side of the bed, Sasha stood with her arms folded across her chest, nodding at two nurses in turn as they pushed meds, placed pads on the chest and warmed up the defibrillator. Her eyes were on the monitor overhead, where green light drew lazy lines across the screen. At some point in the proceedings anaesthesia had shown up and put an endotracheal tube down Mongay's throat; respiratory therapy was wheeling a ventilator to the head of the bed, looping tubing through the bars of the halo and cursing at it.

'Hold compressions,' Sasha said. The nurse stopped pushing on the chest. I saw for the first time that the halo was supported by a broad sheet of plastic backed with sheepskin that covered the upper half of the chest: the nurse had to get her hands underneath it to press; with each compression Mongay's head bobbed up and down, up and down. He was out, his eyes blank at the ceiling. The nurse at my elbow was hooking up the ports of my catheter, pushing one of the blunt syringes of epinephrine. We were all staring at the monitor above the bed, the long horizontal drift of asystole. As the second amp of atropine ran in, the lines all leapt to life, frantic peaks filling the screen.

'V-fib,' a nurse said quietly.

'Paddles,' Sasha replied in the same voice, taking the offered handgrips of the defibrillator from the nurse as she spoke. 'Clear,' she said quietly, and thumbed the button.

John Mongay's body rose from the mattress, hung for a moment, collapsed. On the screen we saw scrambled green light settle for a moment, a rhythm emerge. Then the peaked lines consolidated into a high picket fence.

'V-tach,' said the nurse, and turned up the power on the defibrillator.

'Clear,' said Sasha. The body arched and fell again.

It went on for twelve more minutes, Mongay's heart flying through one arrhythmia after another. Each time we responded it would settle briefly into sinus rhythm before flinging out again into some lethal variation, until finally, after two grams of magnesium sulphate and another round of shocks, it found a rhythm and held it through another flurry of activity when his systolics dropped to the sixties, then rallied on a minimal infusion of dopamine. And through all of this, as the atmosphere in the room maintained its eerie calm, the nurses kept up their surreal economy of gesture, and Sasha intoned the ritual of the ACLS algorithm, I felt my own adrenalin surging through the night's fatigue in an approach to exultation. It was almost beautiful.

This, I thought as we left the room (the lines on the monitor dancing their steady dance, the ventilator measuring breath and time to its own slower rhythm), this is what a code should be. A clean thing. A beautiful thing. The patient hadn't died.

The rest of the night was anticlimactic. There was a note to write (there is always a note to write), for which we had to puzzle some time over the strips churned out by the telemetry system, the notes scribbled on a paper towel recording what drugs had been given when, the values called over the phone from Core Lab and written in black marker on the leg of a nurse's scrubs. There was the call to the family: I had to temper my enthusiasm as I searched for words to use when calling from the CCU at 2.35 in the morning. It was the son who answered. He took the news well enough, asked if I thought they needed to come now. I assured him his father was stable. I assured him everything was under control; I had anticipated the code, I realized, when I moved him to the CCU. He was in the safest possible place. 'In the morning then,' the son said quietly.

'In the morning,' I agreed, and turned to the call room at last, where I spent perhaps forty-five minutes on my back, replaying the code against the springs of the empty bunk above me, until my pager went off again and this time it was the ER. And then around five, another code on 4 West, where we found a man bleeding from a ruptured arterial graft and I had to put yet another catheter in yet another groin, and this time there were fourteen nurses in the room, all shouting at once, so that I had to bellow over them to be heard as I requested, repeatedly, the proper catheter kit, something big enough to pour in fluid as fast as he was losing it. The patient was alive when I saw him last, a scared and tousled surgery intern kneeling right on top of him to hold pressure as the entire ungainly assemblage – patient, intern, and tree of IV bags – wheeled out the door to the OR. Back to normal life, I said to Sasha as we trudged back to the cardiology ward. Whether she knew what I was talking about I couldn't say, and didn't really care. I was still warmed by a vague sense of something right having happened. Mr Mongay had coded, coded beautifully, and he had survived. We had done everything right.

The next morning on rounds, we were congratulated for our management of Mr Mongay's arrest, although there was an ominous pH value from a blood gas obtained early on in the event that occasioned some shaking of heads. He had not responded since the code, being content to lie there unconscious in his halo, his chest rising and falling in response to the ventilator's efforts. But his vital signs were stable, his labs from the 4 a.m. draw were looking good, and I had my hopes. No longer for an early discharge, but I was hopeful, all the same.

I shared these hopes with Mrs Mongay and the family when they arrived at seven. She stood at the bedside looking down, and her eyes were wet, her mouth unstably mobile. She reached out almost to touch the bars supporting the halo, down one of the threaded rods that pierced her husband's skin above the temple, almost touched there, then withdrew her hand. 'Is this the . . . thing? What do they call it?'

I was silent a moment.

'A halo,' I said finally. 'They call it a halo.'

'Ah,' she said.

John Mongay died five days later, having never regained consciousness. As each day passed and he gave no sign of mental activity, eventually it became clear that not all of him had survived the code. The family decided, once pneumonia set in, to withdraw support. Even though I had anticipated the pneumonia, and was pretty sure I could get him through it, I had to agree it was for the best.

He had become something unreal to me — something beautiful, like a work of art, but unreal. Amid all the mess and squalor of the hospital, with its blind random unravelling of lives, in their patient dignity and kindness he and his family stood apart. In his case, for a little while at least, everything had gone exactly as it should have. The perfect code. And it hadn't made any difference. After a bedside service, I pulled his tube early in the afternoon, and took my place at the wall while the usual drama worked to its conclusion.

They sent me a card that Christmas, Mrs Mongay and her daughters. I kept it for a while, until it vanished in the clutter on my desk. She had written a text inside, something from the New Testament I had admired at the bedside service, but soon forgot. I do remember vividly the picture on the card. It was like the Mongay women: sober, attractive. It showed a medieval nativity scene, all saints and angels with their burnished golden ovals overhead. Their faces were sorrowful in profile, as if anticipating what will crown that rosy newborn, perfection laid in straw, with pain in time to come. ■

RACHEL SHIHOR
TRANSLATED FROM THE HEBREW BY ORNAN ROTEM

The Former Mayor's Ancient Daughter

With us in the nursing home lives the ancient daughter of the former mayor, and every week her old manicurist comes to see her, like an emissary from her previous life. To begin with, she softens her twisted nails in lukewarm soapy water, which she carries in an assortment of bottles. This helps peeling off the excess skin; filing down the nails becomes easier too. Afterwards, she will say to her: Pedicure as well? And the former mayor's daughter, whose head resembles a thorny tower, will hold up to her eyes the tiny containers of creams and hair dyes that always overflow from the manicurist's little case. Later on, they will drink instant coffee from the machine. The mayor's ancient daughter will suggest it, and will pay for it too. In the courtyard, right next to the shaded table, they will sip the wonderfully tepid coffee, and for a while it will seem to them that the whole world is in retreat, and before long, no one will be left but them, sitting beneath the broad-leafed mulberry tree, sipping their coffee as if they have nothing save each other. ■

THE THIRD DUMPSTER

Gish Jen

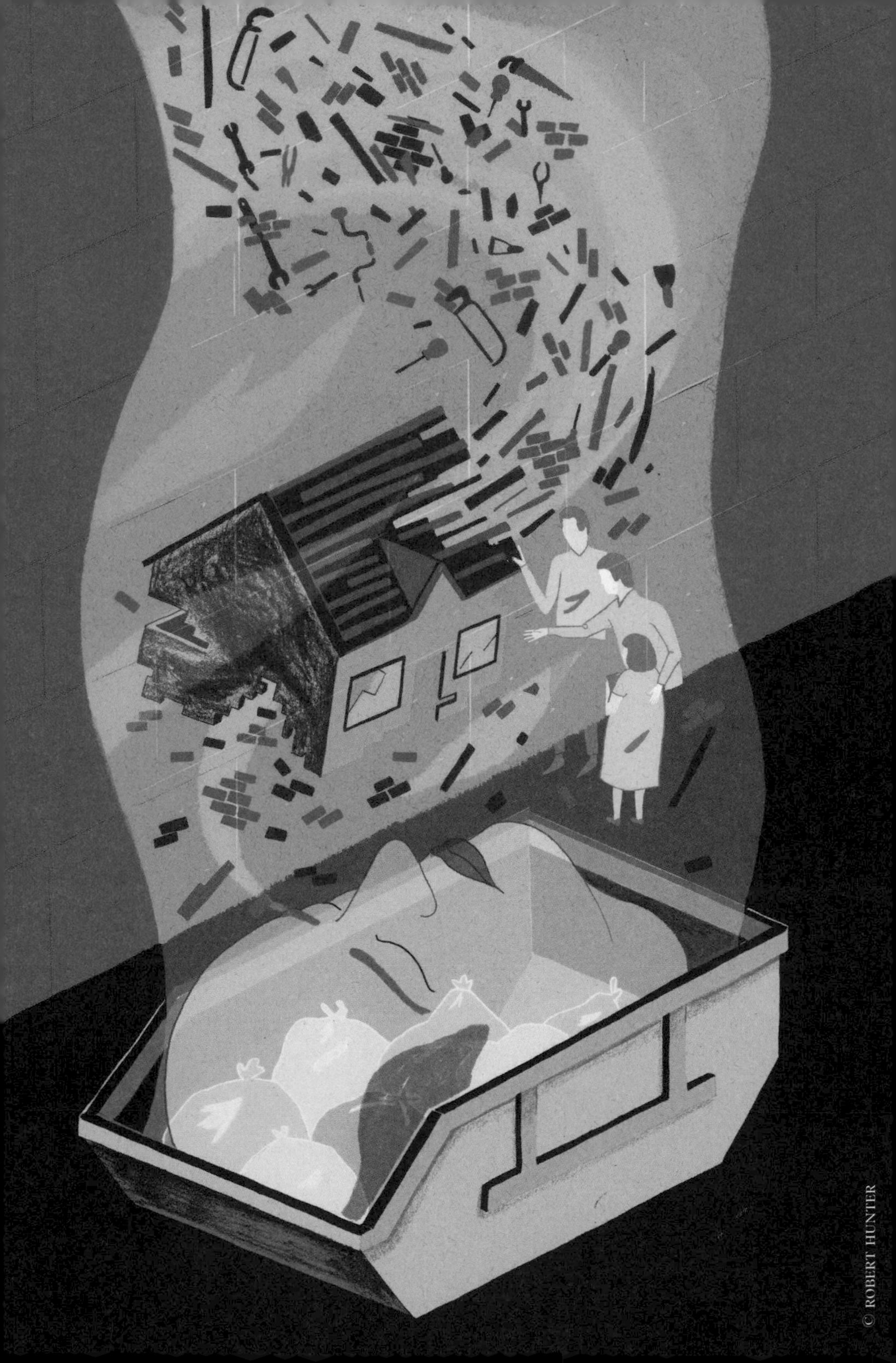
© ROBERT HUNTER

Goodwin Lee and his brother Morehouse had bought it at auction, for nothing. Even the local housing shark had looked down at his list and frowned and pinched or maybe itched his nose, but then waved his hand to clarify: no bid. The house was a dog. However, it had a bedroom on the first floor and was located in the same town as Goodwin and Morehouse.

They were therefore fixing it up for their parents. Goodwin and Morehouse were good with fixer-uppers, after all; they were, in fact, when they were working, contractors. And their parents were *Chinese, end of story,* as Morehouse liked to say. Meaning that though they had been Americans for fifty years and could no longer belay themselves hand over hand up their apartment stair rail to get to their bedroom, they nonetheless could not go into assisted living because of the food. Western food every day? *Cannot eat*, they said.

Goodwin had brought them to a top-notch facility anyway, just to visit. He had pointed out the smooth smooth paths, so wonderful for walking. He had pointed out the wide wide doorways, so open and inviting. And the elevators! Didn't they make you want to go up? He had pointed out the mah-jong. The karaoke. The six-handed pinochle. The senior tai qi. The lobby was full of plants, fake and alive. Always something in bloom! he said, hopefully.

But, distracted as they could be, his parents had frowned undistractedly and replied, *Lamb chops! Salad!* And that was that. His brother, Morehouse, of course, did not entirely comprehend their refusal to eat salad, believing as he did in raw foods. He began every day with a green shake whirled in a blender with an engine like a lawnmower's; the drink looked like a blended lawn, perfect for cows.

But never mind. Morehouse accepted, as Goodwin did not quite, that their parents were fundamentally different; their Chineseness was inalienable. Morehouse and Goodwin, on the other hand, would never be *American, end of story,* which was why their parents had never been at a loss for words in their prime. *You are finally learn how to act! You are finally learn how to talk! You are finally learn how to think!* they had said in their kinder moods. Now, though, setting their children straight had at last given way to keeping their medications straight. They also had their sodium levels to think of. One might not think the maintenance of a low-salt diet could be a contribution to inter-generational peace, but, in truth, Goodwin found it made his parents easier to love – more like the diffuse-focus old people of fairy tales, and less like people who had above all held steadfast against the irresponsible fanning of their children's self-regard.

The house, however, was a challenge. See these walls? Morehouse had said. And he was right. They were like the walls of a refrigerator box that had been left out in the rain. The bathroom was veined a deep penicillin green; its formerly mauve ceiling was purpurating. Which was why Goodwin was out scouting for dumpsters. Because this was what the recession meant in their neck of the woods: old people moving into purpurating ranch homes unless their unemployed children could do something about it. He did not, of course, like the idea of illicit trash disposal; he would have preferred to do this, as all things, in an above-board manner. But Morehouse had pushed up his sun visor, flashing a Taoist ba gua tattoo, and then held this position as if in a yoga class.

Tell me, he said patiently. Tell me – what choice do we have? Tell me.

The gist of his patience being: Sure it was illegal to use other people's dumpsters, but it was going to save him and Goodwin eight hundred dollars! Eight hundred dollars they didn't have between them, four hundred they didn't have each. It was about dignity for their parents, said Morehouse. It was about doing what they were able to do. It was about doing what sons were bound to do, which was not to pussyfoot around. Morehouse said he would do the actual dumping. Goodwin just had to figure out where other people were having work done, and whether their dumpsters were night-time accessible. As for why Goodwin should do the scouting, that was because Morehouse was good with a sledgehammer and could get the demo started. Goodwin was dangerous with a sledgehammer, especially to himself.

Now he scouted carefully, in his old Corolla wagon, eating Oreos. One dumpster was maybe too close, he thought. Might not its change of fill level be linked with their dumpsterless job right around the corner? Another possibility was farther away. That was a small dumpster, though – too small for the job, really. Someone was being cheap. Also, it was close to a number of houses. People might wake up and hear them.

The third dumpster was a little farther away yet. No houses nearby; that was because it was for the repurposing of a bowling-alley. Who knew what the alley was being repurposed for, but an enormous bowling-pin-shaped sign lay on the ground, leaning horizontally against the cinder-block building. It looked as if the pin had been knocked down for eternity and would never be reset. The dumpster in front of it, in contrast, was fresh and empty, apparently brand new. Bright mailbox-blue, it looked so much more like the Platonic ideal of a dumpster than the real-world item itself that Goodwin found it strangely heartening. Not that he would ever have said so to Morehouse, of course. And, in fact, its pristine state posed a kind of problem, as dumping things into an empty dumpster made noise; the truly ideal dumpster was at least one-quarter full. Goodwin had faith, though, that this one would soon attain that condition. The bowling alley was closed; a construction company had put its sign up by the street. There would be trash. It was true that there were street lights nearby, one of them in working order. That meant Goodwin and Morehouse would not have the cover of darkness. On the other hand, they themselves would be able to see. That was a plus.

At the house, Goodwin found Morehouse out back, receiving black plastic bags full of debris from some workers. The workers lifted them up to him like offerings; he heaved them, in turn, into a truck. Of course, the workers were illegal, as Goodwin well knew. He knew too that Morehouse knew Goodwin to be against the use of illegals, and that Morehouse knew Goodwin knew Morehouse knew that. There was probably no point in even taking him aside. Still, Goodwin took him aside.

Did you really expect me to demo this place all by my friggin' self? asked Morehouse. Anyway, they need the work.

The workers were Guatemalan – open-miened men who nonetheless looked at each other before they said or did anything. Their names were Jose and Ovidio. They shared a water bottle. As Morehouse did not speak Spanish, and the Guatemalans did not speak English, they called him Señor Morehouse and saved their swearing for each other. Goodwin remembered enough from his Vista teaching days to pick up *¡serote!* and *¡hijo de la gran puta!* and *¡que vaina!* Still the demo was apparently going fine. Goodwin watched as they delivered another half-dozen bags of debris to Morehouse.

And that's not even the end of the asbestos, said Morehouse.

Asbestos? cried Goodwin.

You can't be surprised there's asbestos, said Morehouse.

And indeed, Goodwin was not surprised, when he thought about it. How, though, could Morehouse have asked Jose and Ovidio to remove it? Their lungs! Goodwin objected.

They want to do it, Morehouse shrugged. We paid them extra. They've got it half in the bags already.

But it's illegal!

We have no choice, said Morehouse. And: They have a choice. They don't have to say yes. They can say no.

Are you saying that they are better off than we are? That they have choices where we have none? That is a gross distortion of the situation! argued Goodwin.

Morehouse looked at his watch: time for his seitan burger.

Dumping asbestos is like putting melamine in milk, Goodwin went on. It's like rinsing off IV needles and selling them back to hospitals. It bespeaks the sort of total disregard for public safety that makes one thankful for lawsuits, as Jeannie used to say.

Jeannie was Goodwin's prosecutor ex-wife – a woman of such standards that she'd been through some two or three marriages since theirs. Morehouse smirked with extra zest at the sound of her name.

You seem to think we have no choice, but we absolutely do have a choice, declared Goodwin then. We could, for example, take Mom and Dad in to live with one of us.

For this was the hot truth; it seared him to say it.

Morehouse, though, gave him the look of a man whose wife brought home the bacon now. It was the look of a man who knew what would fly in his house, *end of story*. He lowered his dust mask.

Did you or did you not find a friggin' dumpster? he asked. His mask was not clean, but neither was it caked with dust, like the masks of Jose and Ovidio. What you could see of their faces looked dull and crackled, like ancient earthworks that had started off as mud.

In the end, Goodwin looked the other way as more bags were filled. And though Morehouse had promised to do the dumping, it was Goodwin, finally, who drove the bags to the mailbox-blue dumpster. At least there was, as he predicted, some trash in it now. He did not make much noise as he threw his bags in deep, where they were less likely to be seen by the bowling-alley crew in the morning. The bags were heavy and shifted as if with some low-valence life force. Still, he hurled them as best he could, glad for the working street light but a little paranoid that someone would drive by and see him. No one did. He did think he saw, though, a bit of white smoke rise from the dumpster as he drove away. That was not really possible. The asbestos was in bags, after all; the bags were tied up. He was probably seeing some distortion in the lamplight. And didn't other things send up dust besides asbestos? Sheetrock, for example. Sheetrock sent up dust. Still, he thought he saw asbestos rising up on that dump, and on another dump he made before switching to yet another dumpster he had found, behind a Masonic temple. He didn't think there was asbestos in any of the new bags of trash, but who knew? He didn't ask, and Morehouse didn't say.

In a further effort to save money, Goodwin and Morehouse roughed out the walls themselves; and though they didn't have an electrician's licence, they took care of the wiring too. They even set a new used cast-iron tub, or tried to. In fact, they got it three inches too high and had to turn once again to Jose and Ovidio for help getting the thing back out. Of course, Jose and Ovidio shook their heads and laughed when they saw what had happened. *¡Que jodida!* they said. Then they spent an entire day grimacing and straining, their faces almost as purple as the ceiling. When the tub finally rested back on a pallet in the hall, Ovidio stared at it a long moment. *¡Tu madre!* he muttered, to which Jose swore back *¡La tuya!*, his arms jerking up and down, his neck twitching with anger. He pulled up his pants, maybe because they were too big; Goodwin made a mental note to bring him a belt, though what Jose and Ovidio probably needed was more food. Would Goodwin have been right to insist, as he wanted to, on finishing the job without them? After they'd already helped with the dirtiest and most gruelling parts? He decided to let Morehouse have his way, and had to admit that Jose, at least, looked happy to have the work. Goodwin gave him a belt, which he seemed to appreciate; he slipped both men an extra twenty too. Take it, Goodwin told them. *Por favor.*

Was this why the work went quickly and well? And yet, still, Morehouse and Goodwin kept their parents from the site for as long as possible, knowing that something about the project was bound to spark their disapproval. *House cost nothing, but look how much you spend on renovation,* their mother might say. Or, *How come even you have no job, you hire other people to work?* Morehouse, naturally, was well stocked with rebuttals, starting with, *Don't worry, we barely pay those workers anything.* What difference these could make, though, was unclear.

Finally, though, it couldn't be helped; their parents came for a visit. They looked around stupefied. The house was not much bigger than their apartment, but it was big enough to make them seem smaller; and all new as it was, it made them look older.

Very nice, said their mother finally. She clutched her leather-trim pocketbook as if to ward off attackers; she showed real excitement about the window in the bathroom and the heating ducts. *No radiators!* she exclaimed. Their father looked as much at Jose and Ovidio as at the house. *Spanish guys*, he said. Jose and Ovidio laughed and kept working. Goodwin tried to explain what they were doing. What the house used to look like. What it was going to look like. And how much they, his parents, were going to like it. It was like trying to sell them on the assisted-living place. Everything on one floor! Close to their sons! Right in the same town! His pitch was so good that Morehouse stopped and listened – suddenly touched himself, it seemed, by what they had wrought. He beamed as if to say, Behold what we've done for you! He leaned toward their shuffling father, as if expecting to hear, What great sons you boys are!

Instead their father tripped over a toolbox and fell as if hit by a sledgehammer. Dad? Dad? He was conscious but open-mouthed and breathing hard; there was some blood, but only, Goodwin was relieved to see, a little. *I fine*, he insisted, flapping a shaking hand in the vicinity of his hip. Your hip? asked Goodwin. Their father nodded a little, grimacing – his brown age spots growing prominent as his real self, it seemed, paled. Don't move, it's OK, said Goodwin. It's OK. And, to Morehouse: Do you have an ice pack in your lunch box?

Morehouse called an ambulance. People said the ambulance service was quick around here, or could be; that was reassuring. As he and his family waited, though, Goodwin stared at his father lying on the floor, and was shocked at how like a house that could not be fixed up he seemed. He stared into the air with his milky eyes as if he did not want any of them to be there and, oddly, covered his mouth with his still-trembling hand. It was a thing he did now at funny times, as if he knew how yellow his teeth were; or maybe it was something else. Goodwin's father had always been a mystery. Now he was more manifestly obscured than ever. The few things he said were like ever darkening peepholes into fathomless depths. *You don't know what old is,* he said sometimes. *Everything take long time. Long, long time.* And once, simply: *No fun.*

His more demonstrative mother cried the whole way to the hospital, saying that his father fell because he didn't want to move into this house, and that she didn't either. It was her way of making herself clear. She didn't care whether or not it was the sort of house a person could live in by herself one day, she said. Chinese people, she said, did not live by themselves.

They were passing the turn-off for Goodwin's house when she said that. Goodwin was glad they were in an ambulance. He smiled reassuringly at his father though his eyes were closed tight; he had an oxygen mask on.

Right now we need to focus on Dad, Goodwin said.

His mother would not take her pocketbook off her lap.

Morehouse, following them in his car so that they would have a car at the hospital, called Goodwin on his cellphone.

If they ask whether Dad needs a translator tell them to fuck off, he said.

Does he need a translator? asked the admitting nurse.

He's lived here for fifty years, answered Goodwin politely.

The nurse was at least a grown-up. The doctor looked like a paper boy.

Does he need a translator? he asked.

Fuck off, said Morehouse, walking in.

How Goodwin wished he had said that! And how much he wished he had ended up like Morehouse instead of like Morehouse turned inside out. For maybe if he had, he would not have sat in the waiting room later, endlessly hearing what his mother wanted him to say – *You guys can come live with me* – much less what she would say if he said it: *You are finally learn how to take care of people. Who knows, maybe next time your wife get divorced, she come back, marry you again.*

Instead his mother was probably going to say, *You know why your wife dump you? She is completely American, that's why. Even she marry you again, she just dump you again. You wait and see.*

Fuck off, he would want to say then, like Morehouse. Fuck off!

But, of course, not even Morehouse would say that to their mother any more. Now, in deference to her advanced and ever-advancing age, even Morehouse would probably nod and agree. Their mother would say, *That's what American people are. Dump people like garbage. That's what they are.*

And Morehouse would answer, *That's what they are, all right, the fuckers.*

Nodding and nodding, even as he went on building. ■

Blueberries

I'm talking to you old man.
Listen to me as you step inside this garden
to fill a breakfast bowl with blueberries
ripened on the bushes I'm planting now,
twenty years back from where you're standing.
It's strictly a long-term project – first year
pull off the blossoms before they open,
second year let them flower, watch the bees
bobbing in every bonnet,
but don't touch the fruit till year three,
and then only sample a handful or two . . .
Old man I'm doing this for you!
You know what they say about blueberries:
blood-cleansing, mood-lifting memory-boosters;
every bush a little fountain of youth
sparkling with flavonoids, anthocyanin . . .
I've spent all summer clearing brush,
sawing locust poles for the frames,
digging in mounds of pine needles, bales of peat moss –
I thought I'd do it while I still could.
You can do something for me in turn:
think about the things an old man should;
things I've shied away from, last things.
Care about them only *don't* care, too
(you'll know better than I do what I mean
or what I couldn't say, but meant).
Reconcile, forgive, repent,
but don't go soft on me; keep the faith,
our infidel's implicit vow:

'Not the hereafter but the here and now . . .'
Weigh your heart against the feather of truth
as the Egyptians did, and purge its sin,
but for your own sake, not your soul's.
And since the only certain
eternity's the one that stretches backward,
look for it here inside this garden:
Blueray, Bluecrop, Bluetta, Hardy Blue;
little fat droplets of transubstantiate sky,
each in its yeast-misted wineskin, chilled in dew.
This was your labour, these are the fruits thereof.
Fill up your bowl old man and bring them in.

UK PUBLISHERS' NOTICEBOARD

The Lair by *Norman Manea*

A literary figure whose works evoke comparisons to such giants as Kafka and Musil, Norman Manea explores the human condition of exile in this acclaimed novel of love, isolation and the disorientation of being submerged in another culture.
Yale University Press £14.99 | HB

Index on Censorship

International in outlook, outspoken in comment, award-winning magazine *Index on Censorship* is the only publication dedicated to freedom of expression. As London got ready for the Olympics, *Index* visited the ethical pit stops, asking whether sporting events can be good for democracy and considering the appeal of championships to sports-mad politicians.
40th Anniversary Subscription Offer: Get all 4 issues of Volume 41 for £17.40
Visit **www.indexoncensorship.org/subscribe** for more details

The Prisoner of Heaven by *Carlos Ruiz Zafón*

First there was *The Shadow of the Wind*, then *The Angel's Game*. Now return to the wintry streets of Barcelona to find out what happens next. *The Prisoner of Heaven* is full of intrigue, emotion and betrayal. Reuniting us with Daniel, Bea and Fermín from the *Shadow of the Wind*, it takes us on a magical journey back to the Cemetery of Forgotten Books.
Weidenfeld & Nicolson £16.99 | HB

Nagasaki: The Massacre of the Innocent and the Unknowing by *Craig Collie*

When the bomb fell on Nagasaki in August 1945, it brought WWII to an end, but it also killed 80,000 people, half of them instantly. Pieced together from interviews, contemporary records and official documents, this is a powerful and unprecedented reconstruction of a devastating historical moment.
Portobello Books £20.00 | HB

PEOPLE DON'T GET DEPRESSED IN NIGERIA

Ike Anya

It is a cold January morning and I am sitting in a cafe on a busy London street. Looking out of the window, I watch people bustle determinedly along the pavement. I remember how my English friends used to complain that I walked too slowly when I first arrived in London. I thought they walked too fast, but now, in the chill of winter, I find myself quickening my own pace and lengthening my strides, eager to get back to warmth. I unfold the newspaper that I've found lying on the table and struggle to keep the still-unfamiliar, outsized pages from encroaching upon the space of the people seated at the tables next to me. I open the newspaper and the word 'Nigeria' catches my eye. It is funny how my mind always, almost unconsciously, seems to seek that word out whenever I am reading a paper. Sometimes I am fooled and the reference is to Nicaragua, but this time my eyes have found a worthy target. It's a feature on the young British Nigerian novelist Helen Oyeyemi in which she speaks of her struggle with depression in her teenage years and the difficulty her parents faced with understanding it. 'Because people don't get depressed in Nigeria,' she says. 'They were like, "Cheer up, get on with it."'

The black words sliding over the page carry me back in time to another place, where I too, like Helen's parents, believed that people don't get depressed in Nigeria.

It has been a hot night; much of it spent rolling away from the concrete against which my bed is pushed. The walls, retaining the fiery, dry heat from the sun of the previous day, burn with an intensity that seems to scorch my skin when, in my fitful sleep, I roll to the edge of the bed closest to them. I have woken up with a start several times, finally dozing off in the early hours of the morning.

I wake up to a clucking sound outside my bedroom window. It is guttural, low-pitched, and there is a rustling in the fields of guinea corn that stand sentry immediately outside our low-eaved modern bungalow. I walk to the window and peer through the grimy glass louvres, past the hole-ridden metal mosquito netting, and see a herd of cattle making its gentle, almost silent way through the fields. In a distant corner, I can see the Fulani herdsman, a boy really – he is the source of the clucking noise. Whenever a particularly adventurous cow threatens to stray too far, he clucks, softly, almost under his breath, yet loudly enough for the sound to carry into my bedroom, and the cow wanders back to the fold. I remember the stories I have heard about Fulani being able to 'talk' to their cattle, and from what I can see, it seems that the tales told by an old driver of my father's who had once lived in the North are true.

I walk out into the living room that I share with the other occupant of the small two-bedroomed house set on the edge of the hospital compound and head for the bathroom. There I retrieve my battered metal bucket and head out to draw the water for my morning ablutions. At the well, there is a gaggle of young children, chattering rhythmically in Hausa as they deftly throw the black rubber *guga* into the well, hauling it up to fill the buckets and jerry cans surrounding it. As they see me make my way along the path lined with bowing neem trees, they shriek their greetings, laughing, excited.

'*Sannu, Likita, sannu.*'

I am *likita* – Hausa for doctor – and I am twenty-seven years old, freshly qualified from medical school in southern Nigeria and posted to this small northern village for my national service.

One of the children rushes to grab my bucket and, despite my protestations, runs to the well to fill it up and deposit it back at my feet. I thank him and head back to the house, leaving the children to continue their chatting and fetching. I walk past the fields planted with cotton, where the first white balls of fluff on the ripened, splitting pods are only just beginning to show. It will be harvest time soon and the village will flourish in the brief prosperity conferred by the sale of their *auduga* to the merchants who send their agents from Kano, the nearest big city.

Back in the house, my housemate Wilson is awake and already dressed. As usual he has chosen to wear the khaki trousers and jacket that is the uniform of the 'corpers', as those of us on national service are called. Like me, he is another fresh graduate – of medical laboratory science – and is in charge of the fledgling hospital laboratory which, in reality, consists of a couple of microscopes, some dusty slides and, in a slight acknowledgement of contemporary times, a handful of HIV rapid-test kits. Coming from a large teaching hospital in Lagos, with a whole plethora of medical equipment, I am struggling to adjust to the austere realities of rural medical practice.

I brush my teeth, using water that we have boiled and cooled in a large pot in the kitchen, and have a quick bath. I dress in *my* uniform – short-sleeved cotton shirt, blue jeans tucked into the sturdy brown khaki boots that we were issued in camp – my only concession to my corper status. Carefully hanging my sunglasses (bought in more stylish times in a traffic jam in Lagos) round my neck, I walk to Wilson's room. Sitting in our single armchair, its cushions worn and holey, I tuck into the plate of hot rice and beef stew that Wilson has conjured up on the small kerosene stove that sits just outside his room. Beef is plentiful, thanks to the Fulani herdsmen. As I go to wash the plates, Wilson bids me farewell and heads out to work. The clinic starts later so I have a bit more time.

I walk down the tree-lined mud path that leads from the grandly named staff quarters to the hospital, pausing on the way as I meet colourfully dressed and veiled women heading for the market in the next village, who greet me in the elaborate formal ritual of the Hausa culture.

Ina kwana . . . ina kwana, I echo as they enquire after my well-being, my work, my family.

Ina gajiya?
Ba gajiya.
Yaya aiki?
Da godiya.

We finish off with a *madalla* and I make my way along the low-ceilinged corridors to the clinic where, as usual, there is a large mass of people of all ages and sexes already gathered. Looking into the distance, I notice that work seems to have started again on the wall that is being built around the hospital by the Petroleum Trust Fund. It isn't clear who has decided that this is what we need most – a generator to stop us doing surgery by lantern light might have been good, as would some equipment for Wilson's fledging laboratory – but the contracts have been awarded in faraway Abuja and Kano, and so I suppose we must be grateful that the contractor at least seems to be making a good fist of building the wall, which is supposed to provide us with additional security. And he has employed local labourers to do it, so we must be grateful for that as well.

Muttering angrily to myself, I settle into my chair and ask Sani, the cheerful youth who, with his smattering of English, has bagged the role of interpreter, to summon the first patient. I hear him calling out a woman's name, having first, with an air of self-importance, bid the crowd to be quiet and to listen well. I have soon learned that everyone who works in the hospital is highly revered in the village. We all, apparently, are called *likita* and there are rumours that the theatre cleaner, the hulking Kaka, runs a thriving sideline in low-price hernia surgeries performed after hours in his living room. Considering how bare the theatre itself is, his living room may perhaps not be that much more under-equipped for the purpose.

A bearded young man, perhaps twenty-five years old, dressed in a blue *riga*, walks into the room, carrying a toddler in one arm and with the other solicitously leading a young woman, a girl really, dressed in the simple wax-print wrapper and blouse with a loosely tied headscarf that is the common dress of all the female folk here. He greets me respectfully but with an air of distraction as Sani ushers the girl into the seat. The young man stands guard beside her, holding the baby and focusing on my face. She sits listlessly, head bowed, silent.

I look at the blank sheet of paper, torn out of an exercise book, that lies before me and serves as a consultation sheet. I ask her name, her age and what has brought her to the hospital. I do not bother to ask for an address, swiftly amending the history-taking technique learned at my medical school in Enugu. Her husband answers as she continues to look down, despondent. He says her name and volunteers that she is perhaps fifteen years old. Having by now spent over a month in the village, I can already pick out his answers from the rapid-fire Hausa without Sani having to interpret and am not surprised that a girl that young is already married with a baby. It is the way here and one of the nurses has explained to me that in their culture a woman is not supposed to see her second menstrual period in her father's house. He cites the Quran as his source and I tell him of the many Muslim northern Nigerian girls that I knew while at secondary school, many of whom remain unmarried and are pursuing careers. He is silent but I sense that he refrains from challenging me out of respect rather than out of any acceptance of my counter-argument. Returning to the patient before me, I ask again what has brought them to the hospital. My question, once Sani has translated, elicits a burst of animated utterance from the man, his wife remaining silent, her head still bowed.

Her problems started, Sani translates, perhaps a year or so ago, soon after the birth of the little boy, their firstborn. She would spend almost the whole day lying on the mat asleep, she had stopped smiling or singing while she cooked, she now cried a lot, and had ceased doing all of her household chores. I can see the concern on the husband's face as he recounts the many ways in which the girl has changed from the cheerful industrious woman he married, to this lifeless bundle of misery draped floppily on the chair beside me. He swears that he has been good to her, that he does not beat her, even though he is only a poor farmer, and I can see it in the newness of her cheap wax-print outfit and in the rows of bangles that adorn her wrists. They have taken her to see a number of traditional healers but the *maganin gargajiya* has failed to work its magic and so, against the advice of his family and hers, he has brought her here to try Western medicine.

My first thought is of post-partum depression and yet my doubts remain. In spite of our psychiatry lectures and placements, the hours spent in the wards and outpatient clinics at the psychiatric hospital in Enugu, many of my classmates, myself included, still look at depression as a largely Western illness. The few cases that we have seen in the clinics in Nigeria have been mostly among the relatively affluent, and so we imagine that it is a luxury for those who can afford to ignore their more pressing immediate problems – what to eat and how to keep a roof over their heads – to indulge in afflictions of the mood.

And so I probe a little more, asking more questions, trying to disprove the evidence of my own eyes. How, I wonder, can a young woman who has grown up in this harsh environment, waking up early to fetch water, cook, clean, farm till late in the day, be suffering from depression?

And yet, the more I probe, the more the husband, through Sani, proffers evidence to confound my theory. I am conscious that time is passing and that there are still a slew of patients to see on the morning ward round and so I embark on more rapid-fire questioning. Is she eating? No, she has had a poor appetite since the illness began and has consequently lost a lot of weight. She has also stopped visiting her friends and family and takes little or no interest in her child or, indeed, in anything.

The more I try to discount it, the more conscious I am that this is looking more and more like a classic case of post-partum depression. I look up from my scribbling on the page and meet the eyes of her husband, staring, his gaze almost boring into my face, his countenance steady, earnest and hopeful. He has come to us against the wishes of his family and the village and I feel that I owe him something. I must not let him down.

Finally, with an inward sigh, I reach for a pile of neat slips of paper, which Sani has meticulously cut up before I arrive, to serve as prescription forms. The recommended treatment for depression is either therapy or medication. Looking out at the fields of guinea corn and the array of young girls squatting on mats selling food just outside the hospital, there is no question that I only have one option. I look through my formulary, flicking through the well-thumbed anti-infective agent section to the pristine antidepressant section, trying to decide which antidepressant might be most easily available in this remote place. The question of going to the hospital pharmacy does not arise as they have struggled in the past to fill prescriptions for simple antibiotics. The few drugs that they now have in stock are courtesy of the Petroleum Trust Fund, set up by our military president, the goggle-wearing Abacha, to ensure that the benefits of petroleum, our country's main export, trickle down to the masses. Knowing the limitations of the pharmacy, I opt for Amitriptyline, the cheapest and most basic of the antidepressants, and ask her if she is still breastfeeding.

'No,' her husband says, she has not really breastfed at all and the baby is being suckled by his brother's wife who has a toddler of her own.

I scribble quickly and hand the paper to the husband, explaining through Sani how the medication is to be taken. I know that he will probably have to send someone to Kano, a good hour's bus ride away, to buy the medicine. I wonder what it will cost him – this is the lean time between harvests. Perhaps he will need to draw on the last few naira saved from the previous year's cotton crop, reserved for the ram meat for the impending Sallah festivities. Or perhaps he will join the throng of supplicants squatting outside the Hakimi, the village head's palace each morning, bringing their needs and concerns.

Whatever the cost, I sense that he is determined to do whatever it will take to restore his wife to him. I pray that I am not sending this young man on a wild goose chase. I ask them to come back in two weeks, fearful of giving a later appointment, just in case I have got the diagnosis wrong. I do not want to leave her for too long on medication she does not need. They leave the room the same way they came in, a ragged chain of three, her battered plastic slippers dragging on the rough concrete floor.

Two weeks later, I am sitting in the clinic again and my head is reeling. Sani is mopping the floor with disinfectant and bleach where the last patient I have seen, diagnosed with HIV, has vomited. This patient also has tuberculosis and has been admitted into the isolation ward on the far side of the hospital compound. A village boy made good in the city of Lagos, he has come home to die of the mysterious illness that has drained his body and inflicted a hacking, bloody phlegm-producing cough upon him. He is emaciated and I know that his chances are poor.

Perhaps we will be able to treat the TB and buy him a little more time. But the virus that is so evidently rampaging through his body will leave him little time or hope. I know that abroad they now have medicines to treat HIV, and my colleagues say you can even get them in Kano, but they cost far more than even this success story can afford and so I have prescribed TB medicine, some Septrin, vitamins and intravenous fluids and sent him to the isolation ward.

I return to my desk and stare out into the distance, marvelling again at how flat the land around is. I imagine that if my eyes were more powerful I could see right across to Kano, for here, unlike southern Nigeria where I grew up, there are no hills or forests to circumscribe your view.

Sani calls the next patient and she marches forward, her gauzy headscarf tied at a jaunty angle. She carries her toddler in her arms, cooing soothingly to him. Behind her is the bearded husband, a broad smile splitting his expansive face. As she takes her seat beside the consulting desk, he falls to the ground, wanting to grasp my feet in gratitude. I ask him to get up and laughingly begin to scribble on her sheet. I do not need to ask if the medicine has worked.

That afternoon, at the end of the clinic and the ward round, I make a futile dash to the children's ward, summoned by a panting attendant – himself dispatched by the nurses – to resuscitate a dying child. Pronouncing the infant dead, I watch as the mother straps her lifeless baby to her back, gathers their belongings and prepares for the long walk home. Her stoicism contrasts so much with the hospitals where I have trained, where often the sudden sharp wailing of a bereft mother marks the location of the children's ward.

Drained, I make my way to Mama Olu's zinc-walled shack, take my place on the wooden benches and order pounded yam and chicken in okra soup.

As I mould the balls of yam and swirl them around the soup, I hear again bushy-haired Dr Chikwendu, one of my favourite lecturers from medical school, intoning by a patient's bedside on a ward round: 'You must always keep an open mind, in this business. Always be ready to be challenged.'

Nearly a decade later, I sit in a white-panelled meeting room, beneath harsh, bright fluorescent lighting. I look out to the rooftops of west London, the arch of Wembley Stadium barely visible in the distance. My colleague responsible for mental-health provision is explaining the challenge of getting more people to use the new 'talking therapy' service for those with low-level mental-health problems. We have invested hundreds of thousands of pounds, but uptake has been slow.

As we debate how to address this, my mind wanders back to a small, bare consulting room, in a hospital in the northern Nigerian savannah, and I wonder how my patient is faring. ■

GRANTA

PHILANTHROPY

Suzanne Rivecca

Days before she met the novelist, Cora went to the library and brought home a stack of plastic-sleeved hardcovers with one-word titles like *Heirloom* and *Ruffian* and *Seductress*. Her favourite was an early effort with an unusually loquacious title: *The Illegitimate Prince's Child*. At first it was unclear who was illegitimate, the prince or his child. It turned out to be both. During the Hep C Support Group at the drop-in, Cora read aloud sentences like 'Evelina knew Rolf would never marry her if she revealed her true station, but having been a bastard himself, how could he inflict the same fate on the unborn child inside her?' She regaled the needle-exchange staff with passages from *Ruffian*, substituting clients' names for the well-endowed hero's. She knew she was being inappropriate but she couldn't stop. She studied Yvonne Borneo's soft-focus author photos and imagined the hilarious incongruity of her vaunted good works – scattering gold pieces to hookers as she was borne down Mission Street on a litter, that sort of thing – and now that the appointed time had arrived for them to meet, she wanted Yvonne Borneo to deliver. She wanted a white mink hat and coat, a thick tread of diamonds across the collarbones, peacock-blue eyeshadow and sharp swipes of blush and impossibly glossy lips: the rigidly contoured, calculatedly baroque opulence of an eighties soap star auditioning for the role of tsarina. And Yvonne Borneo disappointed her by showing up at Capp Street Women's Services in a plain taupe skirt and suit jacket. Her sole concession to decadence was a mulberry cashmere scarf, soft as a runaway's peach fuzz, held in place with a metal pin shaped like a Scottie dog's silhouette.

'Well, you're just a tiny little mite,' was the first thing she said to

Cora. Her voice was butterfat-rich but filmy, like an old bar of dark chocolate that had taken on a grey cast.

The novelist/philanthropist was more vigorous than her wax-figure photographs, and at the same time much frailer. She thrust her shoulders back with a martial bearing when she laughed, which was often, but Cora noticed her hands trembling slightly when they weren't clasped in front of her. Her hair was beginning to thin. She was grandly imperious in a merrily half-ironic way. When Cora offered her a slice of red velvet cake, which she'd read was the novelist's favourite, Yvonne said, 'Bikini season's upon us. I daren't indulge!' Yet she didn't flinch at the posted Rules of Conduct, scrolled in silver marker on black paper, hung above the TV in the main lounge, and frequently amended for circumstance. In the past few months, necessity had compelled Cora to add 'NO SHOWING GENITALIA', 'FLUSH THE TOILET AFTER YOU SHIT' and 'DON'T JERK OFF IN THE BATHROOM'. This last rule was intended for the pre-op MTFs.

Yvonne read the rules from top to bottom, and when she was done she ruffled herself slightly, as though shaking off a light drizzle. Then she smiled brightly at Cora.

'Well,' she said. 'Girls will be girls.'

Cora reminded herself that Yvonne Borneo was not easily shocked. How could she be? Her only child, a girl named Angelica, had stepped in front of a bullet train at twenty, after years of struggling with schizophrenia and – it was rumoured – heroin addiction and sex work, although Yvonne had never confirmed this. She focused on the schizophrenia, referring to her late daughter as having 'lost a battle with a significant and debilitating mental illness'. The foundation she established after Angelica's death, the Angel Trust, gave money to provide mental health care for young women who had 'lost their way' and were at risk of suicide.

Angelica had been the same age as Cora. As teenagers in the same Utah behaviour modification programme for troubled youth, they had known each other slightly. Cora was waiting for the right moment to tell Yvonne this. She tried to engineer an interval of quiet, seated intimacy, lowered voices, eye contact. But Yvonne moved too fast and talked too quickly, asking about city contracts and capital campaigns and annual reports, and Cora needed her money – the money from airport book sales and Hallmark Hall of Fame movie rights and the pocket change of millions of frustrated housewives – so badly she could hardly keep the desperation out of her voice. The city cuts had been devastating.

The Department of Public Health's deputy director, who had set up this meeting, warned her to cover her tattoos.

'Even the ones on my face?' Cora had said.

'I forgot about those. OK, just don't say anything about her daughter being a dope fiend.'

In Cora's tiny office, Yvonne lingered a few moments before the Dead Wall, which featured photographs of kids who had overdosed or killed themselves or been stabbed. None of these photos were appropriately elegiac, since the bereaved families usually couldn't be counted on to give Cora a cute school picture or a Polaroid of the deceased with a puppy. Most of the dead were memorialized in the act of flipping off the camera or smoking a bowl.

Yvonne put a hand to her chin. 'It's so sad,' she said. 'Such a waste.'

'Yes,' Cora said.

'Well,' Yvonne said. She sat down, crossing her legs. 'What do you envision the Angel Trust being able to do for you?'

She asked this without real curiosity, her tone silky, keen and expertly measured as a game-show host's. Cora began to sweat.

'Well, first of all, I wouldn't have to lay off any more outreach staff,' she said. Without realizing it, she was counting on her fingers. 'And there are basic expenses like rent and utilities. And I'd love to increase Sonia's hours – she's the psychiatrist – because we're seeing a lot more girls with serious mental illness out there right now.'

Yvonne frowned. 'Well, the psychiatrist's hours, yes, I can get behind that. But as for the layoffs – it's always our preference that my funds not be used as a stopgap for deficits in government funding. My board prefers not to dispense bail-out money.'

And this, Cora told herself, was why she hated philanthropists. Their dainty aversion to real emergency and distress, their careful gauging and hedging of risks, their preference, so politely and euphemistically stated, for supporting programmes that didn't really *need* help to stay open, but sure could use a shiny new foyer, complete with naming opportunity. This was what she hated about rich people: their discomfort with their own unsettling power to salvage and save, the fear of besiegement that comes with filling an ugly basic need, their distaste for the unavoidably vertical dynamic of dispensing money to people who have none. The way they prided themselves on never giving cash to homeless people on the street, preferring a suited, solvent, 501c3-certified middleman, who knew better. For Cora, the hardest part of running the drop-in was not the necrotized arm wounds, the ubiquity of urine and rot, the occasional OD in the bathroom, the collect calls from prison. It was the eternal quest for money, the need to justify, to immerse herself in the fuzzy, lateral terminology of philanthropy. Over the last ten years Cora had learned that donors don't give a programme dollars to save it from extinction; they 'build a relationship' with the programme. They want 'partners', not charity cases. And deep down, they believe in their hearts that people in real, urgent need – the kind of person Cora once was, and the kind she still felt like much of the time – make bad partners.

Cora cleared her throat. 'Well,' she said, 'increasing Sonia's hours won't do much good if we don't have a roof for her to work under, or a way of bringing clients to her.'

She thought she saw Yvonne stiffen. Cora knew she was terrible at diplomacy. When she got angry she preferred to yell; and if she were in front of the Board of Supervisors or the mayor's staff instead of Yvonne Borneo, she would have. But this woman, this sleek, self-made authoress – that word, with its anachronistic, feline hiss of implied dilettantism, seemed made for her – had to be handled differently. She had no civic obligation to stem disease; she helped at her whim. It had to be some little thing that reeled her in, some ridiculous coincidence, some accident of fate. And Cora remembered her trump card.

There was no time to wait for a transition. She opened her mouth and prepared to blurt something out, something inappropriate and apropos of nothing – *I knew your daughter when she was a dope fiend*, maybe – when a pounding on the gate stopped her. Then a wailing. Someone was wailing her name.

Yvonne Borneo perked up so markedly her neck seemed to lengthen an inch. 'Do you need to see to that?' she said.

Cora excused herself and went to the back gate. It was DJ, a regular client who had come to the door and screamed for her plenty of times before, but never when anyone important was present. Cora had once lanced a six-inch-long abscess on DJ's arm – she'd measured it – and when the clinic doctor pared away the necrotized tissue, bone showed through. DJ had started coming to the women's centre at nineteen, freshly emancipated from foster care, clearly bipolar, and Cora had been trying to get her to see Sonia for seven years. She was twenty-six now and looked at least forty.

Today she looked worse than usual, in army pants held together with safety pins and a filthy tank top that revealed the caverns of scar tissue on her arms, the bulging sternum that seemed to twang fiercely under her skin like outraged tuning forks. When she saw Cora, DJ thrust both arms through the bars of the gate, like a prisoner in stocks, and wept.

'You came to see me when no one else did,' she sobbed.

'OK, DJ,' Cora said. 'OK.'

DJ did this a lot: went back and forth in time. She was talking about when she'd been stabbed by a john two years before and Cora had been the only one to stay with her at SF General, eventually securing her a semi-private room and making the nurse give her painkillers. 'Yeah, she's an addict,' she had snapped at the young woman on duty. 'It still hurts when she gets stabbed.'

Sometimes DJ would recount an unknown past assault, or several, quietly sitting in the corner of the needle exchange and saying, 'He raped me, Cora,' while peering through the twisted vines of her hair. 'I know, hon,' Cora would say. 'I'd cut his balls off if I could.' This always seemed to calm DJ down.

After Cora's sister had a baby and the baby got older and began to speak in lucid sentences, its vocal patterns and flattened sense of chronology reminded Cora of DJ: that tendency to recount, repetitively, in the balanced and slightly bemused tones of a person under hypnosis, past events as though they had just happened. No 'I remember this', just 'Mama dropped a plate and it broke', meditatively, with an air of troubled, grieving reflection. It seemed to her that DJ, like the baby, was stuck in some cognitive cul-de-sac and, unlike the baby, would never develop a perspective layered and three-dimensional enough to find her way out.

Now Cora looked into her wet face and said, 'DJ, I've got someone in there. Someone I'm having a meeting with. If you come back in an hour, when I open the exchange, we'll talk. OK?'

DJ gazed at her. 'An hour?' she said hollowly.

'Yeah.'

The girl's face began to twist and shift like there was something behind it, trying to get out. She slumped forward, forearms still resting on the bars of the gate, and moaned. Cora smelled alcohol and urine.

'DJ, please. One hour. I've got someone who might give us money in there, and I can't just leave her sitting in my office.'

DJ slumped on the concrete, fingers still poking through the grates, and muttered, 'OK, OK, OK.'

When Cora returned and apologized to Yvonne, the novelist said, 'Everything all right?' Before Cora could answer, the screaming started again. DJ was now banging her head against the metal bars of the gate and howling, 'I'm sorry, I know there's a rich lady in there, but I need to come in!'

Cora grabbed her ring of keys and hurried down the hall. It was starting to get dark outside but she could see a wet patch of blood on DJ's lip from the banging. When she unlocked the gate, DJ fell against her, almost gracefully. Cora staggered under the weight and struggled to dig her hands into the girl's armpits, hoisting her up to standing. She lost her grip, and they collapsed together on the concrete floor. The crotch of DJ's pants was soaked through. 'It's just so cold,' the girl slurred. 'It's just so cold out there. I keep peeing myself, Cora.'

Cora took DJ's chin in her hands and looked into her eyes. They were unfocused and dilated, but not fixed. She was just very drunk.

'I can't be out there right now.'

She pressed against Cora. They were entangled now on the floor of the hall, and Cora felt a hot dribble of urine slowly, exhaustedly trickle across the floor underneath their bodies. 'It hurts,' DJ said.

'I think you might have a UTI again, hon,' Cora said. 'Remember when we talked about pissing right after you fuck?'

'She's fancy,' DJ said.

At first Cora thought DJ was going back in time again, but then realized she was referring to Yvonne Borneo, who stood in the middle of the hallway in her grey suit, arms at her sides, projecting the deliberate, neutral composure of a wartime nurse – one of her own heroines, perhaps, kindly but remote and weighted with an incurable private grief.

'Is there anything I can do?' she said.

And so Yvonne Borneo helped Cora haul DJ into the bathroom. It was Yvonne who picked through the clothes bin and found clean pants and a sweatshirt, who went and bought three black coffees at the diner down the block while Cora helped DJ shower. And later, it was Yvonne who sat in the needle exchange with Lew, the volunteer, while the on-site nurse gave DJ a dose of antibiotics and Cora spent an hour trying to find her a shelter bed for the night. It was fruitless. There was nothing.

'What if we book a decent hotel room for her and you take her there in a cab, make sure she checks in?' Yvonne suggested.

Cora shook her head. 'If she's going overnight somewhere, it needs to be a place where people know what they're doing.' She looked down at her lap. 'The only option is to 5150 her.'

Yvonne didn't ask what a 5150 was. She said, 'Well, if the

alternative is to be on the streets . . .' She trailed off. From the exam room came the sound of DJ alternately screaming and sobbing. The sounds were a kind of last gasp, witless and terrifying as the *crunch* before a piece of machinery breaks down for good. Cora stood up and shut the door to her office.

She made the call. Half an hour later, when the paramedics burst in the front door of the drop-in, four big burly men, louder and stompier than necessary in the way paramedics always are – the way anyone is, for that matter, who comes in the guise of eleventh-hour rescuer – and strapped DJ to a gurney, Cora ran alongside the stretcher and told the girl that things would be OK. But she knew this was unlikely, just as she knew her chances with Yvonne Borneo were blown, because the woman had borne witness to Cora's greatest failure, a failure multiplied by the scores of clients just like DJ: girls who could not change. The part of them that knew how to accept help, whatever that part was called – Hope? Imagination? Foresight? – had been destroyed. And what Cora and her staff did for such girls, day after day, felt more and more like hospice care: an attempt to minimize the worst of their pain until death.

Cora stood in the alley after the ambulance took off. It was Friday night and all the barkeeps along Mission and Valencia were dumping empty bottles into recycling bins. The sound of breaking glass seemed gratuitously destructive, nihilistic. She watched a woman walking down Capp Street in a short swingy coat and heels. A car pulled up alongside her and idled. Some idiot from Marin, thought Cora. The woman and the man in the car conferred for a moment, and the woman drew herself up and hurried down the sidewalk, shaking her head, outraged, as the vehicle pulled away.

When Cora came back into the exchange, Lew was alone.

'Where's Yvonne Borneo?' she said.

'You mean that lady? That narc-looking lady?'

'Yes,' Cora sighed. 'She left, didn't she?'

Lew shrugged. 'She left when the paramedics got here. She looked freaked.'

'Did she say anything?'

'Nope. Maybe *toodaloo* or something.' He flapped his wrist.

Cora sat down. 'She did not fucking say *toodaloo*.'

'No,' Lew admitted. 'She did not.'

The first time Cora saw Yvonne's daughter was in Ravenswood's recreation room. They were both fifteen. She remembered Angelica as tall and big-framed and slumped, with choppy bangs and sidelong, slippery eyes, seemingly beyond nervousness and fear, reduced to the passive, grim spectatorship of an inured captive. There was sympathy in the look she gave Cora, but it was neutered, the retroactive ghost of sympathy you have for your own past, stupid self.

One of the other girls asked how long Cora would be staying.

'Not long,' Cora said, scared. Straining for flippancy. 'Two weeks probably.'

Angelica laughed.

'That's what we all thought,' she said. She spoke in Cora's direction but didn't look at her. Cora tried to snag her gaze but it kept floating away, elusive and directionless. Then Angelica turned to leave the room and that's when she said the chilling thing, head down, so quiet and unassuming she could have been saying it to herself. 'Honey,' she said, 'you are *never* getting out of here.'

That night, her first at Ravenswood, Cora cried and sweated in her bed. Every fifteen minutes an aide came in and shined a flashlight on her. She wasn't allowed to talk to her dad on the phone. 'Can't be a daddy's girl forever,' one of the staff told her cheerfully. A dry-skinned, freckled woman wearing a sweatshirt with a grainy Georgia O'Keeffe flower scanned on the front. 'You have a vagina on your shirt,' Cora told her. The woman's mouth twisted into a tight, hurt smirk. 'You need to grow up,' she said. 'I won't tell anyone what you said this time, but you need to start growing up.'

At night, Cora would watch the snow from the tiny window in the Chill Out Room. She'd discovered that if she said things like *vagina* and *penis* and *fuck* enough, she'd get sent to the Chill Out

Room and could be alone and not have to talk to anyone or pretend to be listening. There was no toilet in there, so she tried to limit her beverage intake. The hours stretched on. Cora would sit on the floor, scowling at the aide who came by every half-hour to ensure that she hadn't found an inventive way to hang herself. All the staff on the girls' ward were women, soft and easily hurt but inflexible, vicious in a hand-wringing, motherly way. Turned-down mouths and sad, round faces. If you called one of these women a fucking twat, her eyes would fill up and her voice quaver with genuine injured dignity. Then she would tell you she was very sorry, but you couldn't shower or change your underwear or socks until you apologized and admitted you were wrong. And the terrible thing was, she'd actually *seem* sorry. They were all perpetually cowed by their own brutality, quivering and defeated by the measures they were forced to enact. If Cora was nice to them, they were worse: unpardonably brisk and springy and relieved, presumptuous in their patting and hugging, insufferable in their tentative optimism. Their non-violent and vaguely cutesy demands – that she sing show tunes in the bathroom to prove she wasn't shooting up or purging, that she do three jumping jacks for every swear word uttered, that she participate in a sock-puppet revue dramatizing what she wanted her life to be like in five years – made her want to kill, and she envied the boys, who, it was rumoured, merely got hog-tied and placed in restrictive holds.

When Cora got home after her meeting with Yvonne, she sat on the floor of her living room and did sudoku puzzles for two hours. Then she tried to sleep but couldn't. The apartment was too quiet and she missed her cat, Melly, who had been dead for two weeks. Melly was a soothing, watchful, totemic presence, like a Buddha statue. She had a charming trait of standing on her two back feet for hours at a time, as if this was a restful position, her front legs hanging straight down from her chest, exposing the fur on her stomach, which was wavier and coarser than the rest. Cora and her friends had gathered round and laughed and marvelled and took pictures on their cellphones and praised Melly for being so cute and novel, until the day the vet informed Cora that Melly had advanced bone cancer and the reason she stood on her back feet was that it was the only position that alleviated her excruciating pain. Melly was put to sleep while Cora held her, whispering apologies, and she wanted to get another cat but was afraid of misinterpreting another signal, unwittingly laughing at another decline.

Melly's food and water bowls were still in the kitchen, half full, the water filmed over with bits of fur on the rim, the corners of each room still hoarding tumbleweeds of cat hair. Cora wiped the rim of the water bowl with her thumb. She kept remembering Yvonne Borneo in the bathroom of the drop-in, kneeling on the floor in her taupe skirt, pulling off DJ's army pants with grim, sharpened concentration. In those moments she seemed to have stepped into a transparent sleeve like the plastic sheaths on her novels, an invisible barrier that kept her from getting dirty. Not shying away from the wetness on DJ's pants. Not wincing at the smell. But not registering it, either. At one point, she leaned over DJ, blotting at the girl's bloody lip, and her Scottie-dog pin dinged against DJ's nose. DJ blinked, started, stared at Yvonne as if she hadn't seen her before.

'You're taking my clothes off,' she murmured.

'Yes,' Yvonne said. 'So you can clean up.'

'Oh, God,' DJ moaned. 'Oh, God.' Then she squirmed to one side and planted her hands flat on the floor and vomited, not all at once but like a cat with a hairball, a series of back-arching, rippling convulsions.

'Get it all out,' Yvonne had said.

The phone rang. A man's voice, clipped and high-pitched.

'Is this Cora Hennessey? Of Capp Street Women's Services?'

'Yes,' Cora said.

Someone's dead, she thought. *DJ's dead.*

'My name is Josiah Lambeaux. I'm the personal assistant to Yvonne Borneo.'

'OK,' Cora said.

It was raining. The ride to Yvonne Borneo's house felt needlessly meandering, up and down hills and around curves in the dense foggy dark, the car's lights occasionally isolating a frozen, fleeting image – a hooded man in a crosswalk, head bowed; a shivering sheaf of bougainvillea clinging to a stone wall; peeling layers of movie posters and Lost Cat signs and sublet notices trailing wet numbered tabs, plastered across the windows of vacant storefronts. Josiah drove his dove-grey sedan with the decorous effacement of a dad trying not to embarrass his teenage daughter, and she sat in the back and watched his thin neck tensing, his hands modestly manipulating the wheel with a pointed lack of gestural flair as they entered Seacliff, a hazy Land of the Lotus Eaters perched on the edge of the Presidio's red-roofed orderliness: a mirage of wide, silent streets and giant lawns and strangely permeable-looking mansions, many of them white and turreted and vaporous in the dark, whose banks of windows turned a blind slate toward the bay and its light-spangled bridge. As they turned onto the mile-long, cypress-lined lane leading to Yvonne Borneo's estate, Cora stuck her face an inch from the back-seat window and imagined how hard it would be to run away from this place. Did Angelica break out under cover of night and run the entire mile from the front door to the road? What intricate alarm systems did she have to disassemble before she even crossed the threshold? And once she was free, adrift in this silent, echoing no-man's-land of ghost-houses and yawning boulevards, how did she keep going? Having known nothing but this eerie greensward with its self-contradictory air of utter desertion and hyper-preservation, how did she know where to go, or even how to leave? Cora's own leave-taking, at fourteen, was comparatively easy. She waited until the house was silent and snuck out her bedroom window and climbed the backyard chain-link fence, to the road where her twenty-year-old boyfriend, Sammy, waited in his car. Her father barrelled out the back door after her, chased her across the yard, grabbed the belt loop of her jeans and pulled as she threw herself against the springy fence. She'd been shocked by how easily the fence swayed and shuddered as she clung to it. The change she'd filled her pockets with – pennies mostly – poured out, spattering on the ground and hitting her father in the face and arms. As he clutched her ankle, his eyes were screwed shut against the shower of coins and so he didn't see the foot of her free leg swinging toward him with all the lethal agility of the gymnast she'd once aspired to be, and he could only reel back, shocked, as the heel of her boot stomped down on his face.

She broke his nose. Her poor father who was only trying to protect his little girl from statutory rape at the hands of the druggie boy she adored. The weird sexual territoriality of fathers, some ancient holdover from the days of dowries and bloody marital sheets. Even then, she knew it was about his ego, *his* deflowered honour, not hers. When Sammy overdosed and she came crawling back home, strung out and incoherent, her father wouldn't let her in the house or even talk to her. He sent her to Utah, where Angelica was.

During the moral inventory phase of the twelve steps, she called her father and apologized.

'I'm sorry I broke your nose and put you through all that worry and mess,' she said.

He seemed dumbfounded. 'I don't even like to think about that,' he said. 'As far as I'm concerned, it never happened. You are what you are now, and that's who my daughter is. You. Not that other person.'

'But I have to make amends, Dad,' she said.

He said, 'You can't make amends for something that never happened.'

As the sedan reached the end of the lane and the house reared up before them, Cora forced herself to take deep breaths. Josiah parked and opened the passenger door for her, and she followed him past a row of topiaries and rose bushes, the heads of the flowers bowed by the rain. The house was a giant whitewashed box of sparkling stone, vaguely French Regency, wrought-iron balconies jutting from huge, blue-shuttered casement windows. As she and Josiah walked to the front door, a series of motion-sensor floodlights clicked on, one after the other, dogging their steps.

Yvonne Borneo was waiting for them in the vestibule.

'Cora!' she exclaimed. 'You made it!'

Then she hugged Cora. She wore silk lounge pants and a gauzy tunic, and Cora, chin pressed against the novelist's dry, soft neck, smelled lily of the valley and starch.

'Thank you for having me,' Cora said. During their embrace, Josiah had vaporized; they were alone in a high-ceilinged foyer of slate and marble.

'You are *such* a tiny thing,' Yvonne said, sorrowfully looking Cora up and down.

Dinner was dished out by Josiah: skirt steak and buttered carrots and parsley potatoes in ceramic serving platters. When he produced a bottle of red wine and plucked Cora's glass by its stem, she held up her hand.

'No,' she said. 'No, thank you.'

'It's an excellent wine,' he said.

'I don't drink.'

She'd been saying this for fifteen years, and the reaction was always the same: a wide-eyed, almost abject solicitude as the implications of the statement were processed. Then an abashed hush. Josiah poured her a glass of water.

As soon as Josiah left the room, Yvonne leaned forward slightly and looked at Cora. A centrepiece of bare black branches sat between them. She gently pushed it aside.

'I wanted to have you over to apologize to you, in person,' she said, 'for leaving so abruptly last night.'

'Oh, no,' Cora said. 'No, I understand. I figured you had to get going.'

Yvonne kept gazing at her. 'It was hard for me,' she said slowly, 'to see someone in that condition.'

'Of course,' Cora said.

'How is DJ?'

'Well, they've got her on a forty-eight-hour hold. So . . .' Cora shrugged. 'I guess at least she's detoxing right now. And maybe she'll have a shelter bed by the time she's out.'

Yvonne looked down. 'I don't know how you do it,' she murmured. 'Every single day. How you don't lose hope.'

Cora surprised herself by saying, 'Oh, I do. I just pretend that I don't.'

Yvonne looked up, staring at her sharply, and Cora had a peculiar sensation of loosening, uncurling and pushing off with a fortifying heedlessness that was liberating and bleak. If she still drank, she would have taken a gulp of wine at that moment. In her mind she saw money, coins and coins of it, running through her fingers.

'May I ask you a question?' Yvonne said.

Cora nodded.

'Why did you leave home?'

Cora had told the story of her downward spiral in front of countless donors. After years of twelve-step testimony she could easily slide into the instructive, talking-points tone this spiel seemed to demand. She always began with a disclaimer: *My parents weren't abusive. Which makes me different from most runaways.* Measured, wide-eyed, absolving everyone of everything. *I made a choice.* And she opened her mouth to say it again, and found that she couldn't.

What she heard herself saying instead was, 'I was in love with an older guy, and I wanted to have sex with him.'

Yvonne's fingers closed around the stem of her wine glass. She frowned.

'And that's why you left home?'

'Pretty much,' Cora said. 'My parents didn't let me date. They were really, really afraid I'd turn into a slut. I mean, *preoccupied* with the possibility I'd turn into a slut. As in, every rule they made revolved around protecting me from that fate. And, um, I wanted to have sex. So.'

Yvonne looked grave and slightly stricken.

Cora kept going. 'And this guy got me into drugs, and then he overdosed and I just went crazy. I kind of wanted to die with him. And I think it was mourning, the whole time I was on the street like that. I could say to you that I was a bad, bad girl and experimenting and rebelling, or whatever, but I really do think it was my way of mourning. And I could say there was one big, defining experience that changed me and made it OK, but there wasn't. It's still not OK. It'll never be OK. I just eventually stopped mourning.'

Yvonne said, 'But you got off the drugs. You made a life for yourself.'

'The other thing was a life too.'

Yvonne looked dismayed. 'But what kind of life? Strung out, on the streets? Addicted to drugs?' She trailed off, toyed with her fork.

Cora laughed, meanly. She was suddenly very angry. She had been waiting, she realized, for this chance since the moment they had met. Since before.

'Believe me,' she said. Her voice was deliberate and low, feeling its way. 'No one would do drugs if they weren't fun. The drugs are what I miss the most.'

She laughed again, this time with disbelief at having said it out loud. But it was true.

Yvonne gracefully nudged her glass aside and cradled her chin in one long-fingered hand.

'I wouldn't really know,' she said evenly.

Cora blurted out, 'I was with your daughter at Ravenswood.'

Yvonne stared.

'I don't know how long she was there. I was only there for a month. That's the way it worked, you know, if your parents couldn't afford to keep paying, they'd get told you were cured. And if your parents were rich enough, you were never cured.'

In the dimness Yvonne's face seemed to tighten into facets, like a diamond, each outraged angle giving off light. And Cora kept going. She couldn't stop.

'That place was, excuse me, a mind fuck. They made up a diagnosis and made you try to fit it. Which may have been what they did to Angelica. Who I only saw once or twice, because I was stuck in a tiny padded room, alone, most of the time.'

Her voice was unrecognizable to her ears: ragged, lashing, corrosive. Almost breaking. When she yelled at City Hall, it was mostly a put-on: she was angry, but she also knew she had to seem sane, galvanizing, in the right. Now she was simply ranting. Ranting at the millionaire who had invited her to dinner. And she couldn't stop.

'I was a junkie when I went in there,' she said. 'Like your daughter. And as soon as I got out, I couldn't *wait* to go do some drugs. I felt *lucky* to be out of that place and doing drugs again.'

She was out of breath. For years she had counselled parents, engineered reconciliations, built bridges for girls to reconnect with their estranged families. Even if those families had made terrible mistakes, like sending their daughters to offshore boot camps, beating them, disowning them for getting raped or pregnant. No matter how awful the parents had been, they clung to Cora; they called her and told her how much they loved their daughters. They said things like, 'You don't have to tell me where she is; just tell her that I love her.' They cried. They listened to her with the chastened raptness of converts. They did what she suggested. And if their daughters came back, or pulled themselves clear and forgave their parents, Cora thanked God she'd been patient, bitten her tongue, refused to say the very things she was now saying to Yvonne Borneo.

Yvonne picked up her napkin.

'Let me stop you right there, please, Cora,' she said. Her voice was calm.

'I still –'

'Please,' Yvonne said. 'Please.'

She waited until Cora became uncomfortable enough with the silence to sit back, with poor grace, and say, 'All right.'

'I think,' Yvonne said, 'I wanted to meet you because I knew something about your past. I knew you were a runaway. And on some level I wanted to see you and find out about you. I wanted to find out why you survived and my daughter didn't.'

She folded her hands and cleared her throat, and when she resumed speaking her voice slackened, sagging with the dead weight of futile certainty. 'It's because she was schizophrenic, that's what you'd tell me. And maybe you'd be right. But let me ask you this. If the situations were reversed, if you had been the one to die, and if

Angelica were sitting in front of your parents right now and saying how awful Ravenswood was, what a mistake they made, what would your parents tell her?'

Cora's mouth was parched. The bitten shreds of her lips stuck together when she tried to separate them.

'I don't know,' she said.

Yvonne's mouth stretched into a desolate smile.

'I'll tell you,' she said. 'They'd say exactly what I'm about to. They'd say, "My daughter was an ocean underneath an ocean." And it would be true. I see these girls on the streets, girls like DJ, the girls in your drop-in, and I know every single one of them is someone's daughter. And to their own parents, every single one of them is an ocean underneath an ocean.' She tapped her index figure on the table in rhythm with the words. 'Fathoms and fathoms deep. A complete mystery. My daughter is completely unfathomable to me. And certainly, if I may say so, to you.'

Cora balled her fists under the table. She knew she should be mollified – if this were a TV show, she would be cowed before the unassailable authority of maternal privilege – but she was furious, burning, convinced that nothing had ever made her angrier than this: this artful abdication of responsibility, this consigning of every lost daughter to a communal slag heap of pretty Persephones. She remembered her father's voice on the phone, telling her, 'You can't make amends for something that never happened.' How matter-of-factly he had absolved her of everything. How she wished she could accept his words as a gift and pretend they didn't feel like a swift and brutal erasure of her entire adolescence as though it were some wartime atrocity, a stack of bodies to be buried and sprinkled with lime. He had excised a part of her to the cutting-room floor. And when he reminisced about her growing up, as he occasionally did on her birthday and when he'd been drinking late at night and watching sentimental films on American Movie Classics, he selectively focused on those childhood behaviours that predicted and explained Cora's choice of career. How she'd always had a charitable bent. Defended smaller children from bullies. Brought home injured baby birds. Cried when starving Ethiopians were on the news. A Florence Nightingale whitewash, obscuring the simple fact that she cared about homeless junkie underage prostitutes because she used to be one. She knew what it was like to be Angelica, in a way Yvonne Borneo could never know.

'My parents,' she said, 'would never say that. Because I am not the same person as your daughter. I don't look at what happened to Angelica and think *there but for the grace of God go I.* We're all different. We're all different people!'

She was sputtering now, losing her eloquence, letting herself go in a way she never had before, and in her mind she saw the drop-in shuttered, saw herself somewhere else, working in an art store, maybe, or walking the streets of a strange city, or telling an entirely new subset of people what she used to be and what it meant, giving it a new spin, all the dead and dying girls of the Mission as distant and abstract to her as Bosnian war orphans, as famine victims, far away and someone else's problem, and she remembered how, at the moment the phone rang in her apartment the night before, there was a panicked, nonsensical moment in which she thought, she *knew*, it was Angelica. It was Angelica, calling to tell her something about her mother. To say be gentle with her, because she's in pain. Every moment of the day she's in pain. And Cora lifted her eyes from her plate and said, 'You're not going to give me any money, are you?' When her voice shook, she didn't know if it was with despair or relief.

Honey, you are never *getting out of here.*

She was dimly aware of the thin and careful form of Yvonne Borneo getting up from her chair and walking around the table. Then there was a hand on her shoulder – experimental, inquisitive, in the manner of a cat testing its balance on some unfamiliar surface.

Cora peered through her fingers. The novelist's face was inches from her own. Her brown eyes were very still and steady. Cora knew she was being shown something, that Yvonne was allowing some skimmed-away sediment to settle and collect in her dark eyes, in the grooves of her face, in the curves of her mouth. The look she gave

Cora conveyed neither reproach nor remorse. What did it convey? Cora would never really know. She could only register something old and muddied and orphaned between them, a helpless moat of transference, brimming with the run-off of two people whose primary identities were, in the eyes of each other, not that of philanthropist and beneficiary, or writer and caregiver, but of someone else's mother and someone else's child. And it was this – this ancient ooze of crossed signals, this morass of things unsaid – that made Cora lower her forehead to Yvonne's shoulder and whisper, 'She loved you. I could *tell* that she loved you,' as the novelist stroked her hair the way Cora once imagined her stroking the head of a fox stole, automatically, with the phantom tenderness of a hand toward an object that is not the right thing at all, but is soft at least, and warm. ■

RANDY AND MUMMY AT THE DRAWBRIDGE

Linda H. Davis

If you live near Lunenburg, Massachusetts, in northern Worcester County, you might have seen us at the puppet show: a greying, self-conscious woman and her giggly adult child. About once a month, when the Drawbridge Puppet Theater changes its show – from *Jack and the Beanstalk* to *The Frog Prince* to *Rumpelstiltskin* and so on – my 26-year-old son and I make the ten-mile drive along the winding back roads from our home to attend a performance. Mindful of obstructing the view of the toddlers and preschoolers who come with their parents, we always sit in the back row. And yet we can't hide: the child with the three-day whiskers who claps loudly for all the puppets attracts wondering stares from the Baby Gap crowd.

As we wait for the curtain to part in the middle of the cardboard castle, where fuchsia morning glories climb the pink brick walls, Randy babbles to himself in his sing-song, repeating words and phrases that have nothing to do with the show. Sometimes he presses one hand to an ear, as though he is receiving messages. More for my sake than anyone else's – this place is full of babies and little kids and is highly Randy-friendly – I tell him to keep his voice down. 'Keep your voice down,' Randy echoes.

At curtain time Mr Paul walks in front of the stage. He tells the children about today's show, involving them with easy questions. 'How many stepsisters does Cinderella have?' 'Is there a witch in this story?' Little hands shoot up; children call out answers. 'Yeessss!' says a loud voice from the back of the room. 'Excellent, Randy,' Mr Paul acknowledges with a kind smile. Heads swivel toward us.

Mr Paul explains the difference between puppets and marionettes, and tells us which to expect in today's show. In his gentle, Mr Rogerslike way, he reminds us that the show is only make-believe: there is nothing to be afraid of. 'Clap, laugh, and don't be afraid,' he says.

'No, we hope not,' says Randy in a solemn, low voice.

Looking back at Randy during the first performance we attended six years ago, I see no trace of the traumatic year he had just lived through. On the contrary, he was excited about his birthday that summer and winning the rights and privileges his sister now enjoyed. Though he seemed to accept that he wouldn't be driving a car or following Allie to college, he understood the truly important thing about turning twenty-one. 'Be a man soon,' he said in his loud, Jerry Lewis voice. 'Drink lots of beer, wine, Chardonnay and champagne.'

From the moment the puppets bounced onto the stage – big, odd, dimensional – Randy had been transformed. His babbling ceased. His face, so often distorted by autism's siren song, became the handsome face it should have been. The face I had often looked on while Randy was sleeping. The face that had turned girls' heads until they realized something was wrong with him. Here in the puppet theatre Randy was fully present: not as a twenty-year-old man, but as a normal boy of three or four, who still believed in magic. He smiled; his lovely grey-blue eyes danced. In this theatre of make-believe, Randy became a real boy.

This is the story of our last six years – years that Randy, a human calculator, may some day include in his tally of the last years Mummy was alive, the last time I took him to the puppet show. 'A Sunday,' he will note. It is the tale of how an autistic boy became a man, what he lost along the way, and what adulthood now means for him and his ageing parents, who live together in a pumpkin-red colonial set in a forest of wetlands.

Though Randy has never forgotten our first house – 'Don't have to forget it,' he says excitedly – or the day we finally sold it ('on September 28, 2002, a Saturday') after six years of renting it out – his sense of home is fixed. We moved from our house on Boston's South Shore to our home north-west of Boston 'on June 26, 1996, a

Wednesday, before we sold the old house', Randy says. In the framed watercolour Randy painted for an elementary-school assignment, the red house has purple windows, a purple roof and a block of dark turquoise in the red-brick walkway. A light green starburst alongside the chimney connotes the hemlocks rising around us; in the attached two-car garage is the suggestion of a heart. The downstairs glows in yellow lamplight.

Now picture another house. It is a ranch, with a carport instead of a garage – and it is actually two houses, with a family living in each half – exactly like all the other houses on the army base at Fort Rucker, Alabama. Colour it drab brown. The year is 1961. Here I lived with my mother, my father, my younger brother, Johnny, and our dog, a boxer we named Bama for Alabama.

In my bedroom at the back of the house I sometimes had tea parties with Bama, who allowed me to dress her in my baby clothes and paint her toenails red with Mama's polish. Though she was full-grown, she sat on one of the child's chairs at the little table – at least to a point. 'Pat, I just saw Bama running down the street in a dress and bonnet,' a neighbour told my mother on the phone. 'Yes,' Mama said with a laugh. 'Linda's been having a tea party.'

But now the house is dark. The only light source is the headlamp on the helmet of an army MP patrolling the premises all through the night.

Though we hadn't lived there long – as an army family, we were always moving – I remember being happy. There were afternoons at the lake, picnicking and waterskiing and riding in the boat we shared with another army family. And Daddy was not only the handsomest man in the world (in his white dress uniform, he looked just like a prince); he made me feel very loved. That my mother was also glamorous and a beauty – an Elizabeth Taylor type with dark hair, red lipstick and tinkling gold-coin jewellery – is not significant. She is there and yet curiously absent in my memories of this time. It was Daddy who made life magical. Daddy who got down on the floor and played with us and gave us piggyback rides. He himself was 'a big kid', said Mama. He taught me how to swim. After dinner, he sat next to me at the linoleum kitchen table, helping me with my arithmetic homework, which was painfully hard for me. He spent months working on a Christmas present for Johnny: a big board on which an electric train wound through villages dotted with bright red and yellow trees dressed in New England fall foliage, unlike the trees in Alabama. The time I was miserably confined to bed with the chickenpox, Daddy entered my darkened bedroom and put the warm puppy who was Bama on my bed – an early Christmas surprise.

I was Daddy's girl. And he never just stood or sat next to me; he encircled me. With his big arms wrapped around me, cuddling me, I felt special and safe. There was no reason to be afraid.

And yet in the week running up to 5 March 1961, I found myself thinking terrible thoughts. I imagined that one of my parents would die. The idea came to me after my close girlfriend on the base hurt my feelings. I thought about my parents dying and then wouldn't she be sorry she had said such a thing. But the thought of Daddy dying made me flinch inside, as though someone had hit me.

It was Saturday night and my parents were having a party. There was nothing unusual about that. They often barbecued and danced to records on the patio behind my room.

As wonderful as Daddy was, he was also a tease, and I was overly sensitive and easily hurt. And so when at the party Daddy teased me about something, then waited for his goodnight kiss, I made a point of kissing one of the other officers goodnight instead of him, then flounced off to bed. Daddy laughed.

I woke the next morning in the dark to the smell of smoke and the sound of my parents shouting at me to stay in my room and not open the door: Daddy would come and get me. The house was on fire. My bedroom was down the hall from my parents' bedroom and Johnny's.

After Captain Harbert across the street came to my window and pulled me out of the room, I waited and worried about Bama. Mama and Johnny were at the Boyles' house next door to our house; I was across the street with the Harberts and their daughters. *My dog, my dog*, I kept worrying aloud. *Where's my dog?* I have no recollection of the moment, but I learned later that Mrs Harbert came into the bedroom where I was waiting and told me that my father had died in the fire, and Bama had died too. ('Not my *father*,' I said.) I do recall standing in their carport, wrapped in the sheltering arms of Captain and Mrs Harbert, and watching the firemen carry a covered stretcher out of our burned and gutted house, then lift it up into the ambulance and out of sight. By then, I knew about Daddy and Bama, but I was confused: surely whatever was under that lumpy, shallow blanket could not be my big father. And where was the stretcher for my dog?

Back home in Portland, Oregon, I was sitting in a chair in my grandparents' familiar, cluttered apartment – my family's second home during our first years when Daddy had been in Korea – when I finally and forever understood how Daddy died. Years later, my mother said that she had been keeping the newspapers from me and instructing everyone to do the same. But now Grams, Daddy's mother, to whom I had always been close, though not as close as I was to my grandfather, dropped the newspaper article with my father's picture in my lap. The formal portrait of Daddy in his uniform was the same picture my grandparents kept in a big frame in their living room, along with several others of Daddy and Johnny and me. Daddy was their only child. After the fire I realized that now they had only Johnny and me. The article in the *Oregonian* said that Lt Davis was attempting to rescue his daughter, Linda, when he was overcome by the flames and died.

And so it was all my fault.

Daddy was twenty-nine when he died. I was eight, and I knew, as each remaining strand of my world unravelled, falling in charred black wisps in the little room around me, that my life would never, ever be the same.

Even after I was married, at the age of twenty-eight, I vacillated about having children. I worried about being a good mother, worried that Chuck or I would die, leaving our children. But as my third year of marriage approached I wanted a baby, and in 1984, at age thirty-one, two years older than my father had been when he died, I gave birth to a perfect and beautiful daughter, whom we named Alexandra and called Allie. I felt strongly about having two children, not one, as my Davis grandparents had, and having them close enough in age so that they could play together, as Johnny and I had done. Randy – named Randall Davis Yanikoski for my father, John Randall Davis, who had also been called Randy – arrived less than two years after his sister. He too seemed perfect.

Like all autistic children, Randy claimed more than his fair share of his mother's attention. Allie, who had enjoyed my full consideration for her first two years of life, felt angry and resentful.

A series of snapshots from those early years: Randy in his later infancy, a papoose on my back as I wash dishes, fold laundry and walk around the house – a strategy to keep him from crying. Movement calmed him by addressing the sensory deficit so common in autism, but the golden-curled, two-year-old Allie, gripping a stuffed polar bear under one arm and a buffalo under the other, would not have understood that. There were the months before Randy started school at age three, when my racing him in and out of Boston for an early language class at the Children's Hospital inevitably led to a day I got stuck in traffic while rushing back to pick Allie up from kindergarten, and found her orphaned on the sidewalk, her grey-blue eyes and rosebud mouth swollen from crying. There was the month I spent toilet-training Randy so that he could go to school in underwear instead of diapers – a twenty-four-hour-a-day campaign. The summer his words began to come and take root – prompted by my carefully detailed pencil sketches of everything in the house he might ask for, from Diet Coke to a fork to his big stuffed brown bear, Felix. My labelled drawings for Randy papered the kitchen cabinets, turning the kitchen into a classroom. Allie, meanwhile, produced a drawing of her own. One day the social worker who was leading a group for elementary-school siblings of disabled children showed me Allie's crayoned portrait of her family: Papa, Randy and Allie. Mummy was notably absent.

In our long journey together, Randy and I had often seemed separate and alone – two apart in a family of four. Though Randy liked other people and was clearly connected to his family, he was not imperilled by their absence. Allie went away to college, then moved so far away you had to take a plane to get there. Chuck – always an attentive presence in Randy's life, who had spent more time with him than most fathers spend with their children – was later hospitalized. As long as Randy knew they'd be back, that he'd see them again at Thanksgiving, or Wednesday, he seemed unperturbed. But his attachment to me was open and unfiltered, like that of a very young child. To Allie's great disgust, he would appear downstairs in his pyjamas – now an adolescent with hair on his chest – and ostentatiously kiss me on the cheek – ignoring everyone else in the room as he said, 'Goodnight, Mummy!' – giggling, then darting off in his stiff, sliding way, like a big wind-up toy. We began calling him Little Oedipus.

Weekdays were filled with school and work, where Randy was learning to be a medical-records filer – a job that used his superb memory and his savant-like gift with dates. He had been working very efficiently with a school supervisor, at three different locations, including our family doctor's office and a small business. He seemed to be on his way, headed for a meaningful job, a life after twenty-two – the age at which the young disabled in the US lose the federal protections of the Individuals with Disabilities Education Act (IDEA), which includes transportation.

Late in the afternoon of 29 March 2006, Randy accompanied Chuck and me to the emergency room of the Emerson Hospital in Concord, Massachusetts. When it became clear that we were in for a long wait, Chuck phoned our close friends in town, Ann and Gary, who picked Randy up and took him to their home.

I was in renal failure, my kidneys hammered by tumours the doctors were sure were a form of lymphoma. I would need stents put in the kidneys and would have to spend at least a few days in the hospital. By the time I was wheeled away to the operating room, it was almost 9 p.m. Chuck had to leave to pick Randy up and get him to bed for school the next day.

'No Mummy die, no Mummy die,' Randy said as they drove west on Route 2 without me. For all Randy's limitations, he understood the meaning of death. Nine years earlier, he had visited his paternal grandmother at another hospital. Months later, he saw her at her wake. He approached the casket. He tried blowing on Grandma, then touching her. And then he got it. Grandma, he said later, was 'in the box'. Anyone who died was in the box and was never seen again.

After I entered the hospital, Randy refused to visit me. So I wrote him a note telling him he didn't have to visit; he would see me when I got home. I loved him and I would see him soon. That smoked him out. But the timing was lousy. Just before Chuck and Randy arrived in intensive care on my second day there, I had fainted – not once, but twice – after telling Dr Ewa Niemierko, the very kind oncologist who had caught my case the night I came into the ER, what had been worrying me.

'Am I going to die – *next week*?' I asked. When I came to, the curtain was drawn across my room. My friend Ann was sitting by my bed, holding my hand. Chuck was talking to Dr Niemierko on the other side of the curtain, while Randy hovered nearby. I don't know what he heard. But when he finally entered my room – indirectly, like a small aircraft jerked off course by a high wind – he wouldn't meet my eyes. I was limp and pale; IV lines streamed from my bandaged arms. Randy must have seen a rag doll resembling Mummy in the bed. Someone headed for the box.

Within days we had the diagnosis, the prognosis, and the second opinion, confirmed by a lymphoma specialist at the Dana-Farber: non-Hodgkin's lymphoma – the wrong kind. When I pressed the specialist for the prognosis, she wouldn't answer until she'd asked me three times whether I was sure I wanted to know. I said yes: I had a twenty-year-old autistic son at home and I had to know. The oncologist had given me a median lifespan: an additional seven to nine years.

Randy was in school that day and was thus spared the sight of his mother sobbing in the car on the drive home. But Randy had absorbed enough, and would observe enough in the weeks and months to come – Mummy resting during the day, under a blanket on the couch; Mummy unable to drive the car and take him places – to feel profoundly, achingly threatened.

'How're you feelin', Mom? Are you feeling OK, Mom?' he would ask. If I was upstairs in bed, he was even more rattled. 'Mummy's sick,' Chuck told him when he returned home in the late afternoon.

'Still alive,' said Randy.

Or he would be talking about something altogether different and suddenly say, 'Not going to Emerson Hospital. Yet.'

Chuck and I sat down with the social worker from the Department of Developmental Services, and talked about moving Randy to a state-funded group home – not right away, but perhaps in the next several years. I cried and cried at the thought of giving him up.

Reality crashed in on Randy, bringing forth a profoundly shaken boy – a boy whose hands actually shook, whose voice trembled with fear when I gently introduced the idea of his some day living somewhere else, not home.

Now, instead of focusing on the filing he had been trained to do so well at the Lahey Clinic in Burlington, he talked about his mother being sick. Though he was always in school when I had chemo and never again had to see me hooked up to an IV, though I never lost my hair, he knew that I could die.

Any whiff of the hospital hit Randy hard. He kept asking Chuck and me to promise that I'd never go back. But we couldn't promise him, and we couldn't spare him altogether. During my lengthy course of treatment, which spilled into a second year and included surgery, Randy often had to come home from school and immediately get in the car with Chuck and ride back across Route 2, from which he'd just come on the Special Ed van, to pick me up at the hospital. There was no one who could stay home with him.

It took months of reassurance, months of seeing Mummy become Mummy again, before Randy recovered his equilibrium.

We celebrated Randy's twenty-first birthday at the Drawbridge Puppet Theater, where family and friends gathered for a private performance of *Cinderella* followed by cake and ice cream. A few days later, on his actual birthday, Randy did what any normal American kid would do: when his parents weren't looking, he broke into the refrigerator, drank several glasses of wine and beer in rapid succession, and threw up. In his literal-minded way, he had refused all offers of alcoholic sips before then, waiting until the very day he turned twenty-one. He appeared in Chuck's home office making faces in front of the mirror over the fireplace. 'I am so funny,' he said, laughing hilariously.

Then Randy found love. At a Saturday farm programme for adolescents and young adults with autism, he met an exotic-looking girl of Chinese-Yankee heritage named Elizabeth. One day, having shown no special interest in her, Randy hugged her goodbye in his stiff-armed way, kissed her on the cheek, embraced and kissed her mother in exactly the same way, and announced as we headed for the car that Elizabeth was his girlfriend. 'My partner,' he added.

There followed a peculiar romance. Sitting alongside her date in the back seat of the car, Elizabeth wore headphones and listened to music while Randy talked to her mother. During their daily cellphone chats, Randy asked to speak to Elizabeth's mother, or, if Elizabeth was on the way home from school, to her bus driver – both women being better sources of information for the lists of names and birthdays and anniversaries Randy collected, typed into his computer and memorized. He seemed to have no sexual interest in Elizabeth. The day she flirtatiously blocked his view during a video of the Rodgers & Hammerstein *Cinderella* at our house, Randy craned his neck around her to see the movie. When she rose from the couch to pull up her capris, which had slipped down and exposed the crack of her behind, he barked, 'Elizabeth! Sit down!' Left to their own devices, they soon drifted off into separate rooms and closed the doors.

'I am not engaged to Elizabeth, I am not married, I have no children,' Randy said in the new refrain, which asked for reassurance.

'No. You're not engaged, and you don't have to get married or have children. You can have a girlfriend without getting married,' I told him.

And the truth is that for Randy it was mostly the idea of having a girlfriend that mattered. 'You don't have to touch her,' he said, meaning 'I', with obvious relief. He was as proud of this prize as he was of the ID card that allowed him to order a beer or a mai tai (along with a Diet Coke with two cherries, two lemons and two limes, and water with the same) at a restaurant. Though he had never been left home alone, and knew that he would not be following Allie to jobs in Maui and Montana, he was conscious enough of the world around him to want to claim his place in it, and belong.

'I have no family-in-law,' he continued. 'Mummy and Papa won't be there,' he said, as he began to describe an imaginary wedding reception.

And then, as suddenly as she had appeared, Elizabeth essentially disappeared – lost to an all-consuming illness, which kept her largely housebound for eight months. Though Randy and I visited weekly, Elizabeth was no longer able to visit us or attend movies and puppet shows.

An indifferent suitor at best, Randy was nevertheless upset. This seemed to have little to do with the endearing Elizabeth and everything to do with change. Though he had come a long way from his rigid early years of temper tantrums and squealing, mouse-like 'Eeeee! Eeeee! Eeeee!' protest sounds, change remained hard. Elizabeth was his girlfriend: this was a fact, like a birth date or anniversary. It was incontrovertible, carved in a faraway place to which I did not have the pass key. As the months wore on and I endlessly explained that Elizabeth was sick and couldn't help it and that I didn't know when she would be able to go out with us again, Randy grew frustrated. He had a girlfriend, and he wanted to go places with her, not Mummy. (It didn't matter that their dates were chaperoned.) Her illness was an inconvenience, an irritation, an unacceptable change in plans. But it was not truly threatening. Perhaps because she wasn't hospitalized or in bed, Randy never seemed to worry that Elizabeth's life was in danger. He did not associate her illness (which was not cancer) with mine.

As the lost princess kept to her tower, held captive by an undiagnosed illness, Randy and I returned to the puppet show alone. Life in the pumpkin-red house surrounded by wetlands – a house that had been gutted by fire and rebuilt about three years before we bought it – found its new normal.

Randy seemed to forget that I had been sick. Only I lived with the picture of the witch turning over the hourglass.

I also lived with the feeling that I was somehow responsible for my illness. I had done something to trigger it; I hadn't behaved as I should have when the first symptoms appeared. Randy, forever a child, would lose me as I had lost my father, and I could do nothing to prevent it or help him cope.

Those first months after the diagnosis, I had awakened from sleep feeling trapped inside someone else's body – transplanted, as in a horror movie. Until cancer, I had always been healthy and strong. Now, drugged and reeling, wearing Depends because of the stents, I was wrenched by feelings of stupidity and guilt. How could things have gotten so far out of hand? How could I – a sensible woman who never missed annual check-ups, who had regular mammograms and a first colonoscopy – have landed in hospital with renal failure? I might have spared Randy, spared Chuck and Allie (who was on the verge of graduating from college) and saved my kidneys – ultimately I recovered 50 per cent function in one; the other atrophied – if I had caught the disease earlier. How could I have been so stupid?

Like a defence attorney in a court of law, I laid out the evidence to a jury of one: the first subtle appearance of the disease had arrived when I was under intense pressure to finish a book years overdue. Much as Randy's autism had come into view after his first months of life – when he would begin acquiring language and seem to develop, only to lose the words and slip back – cancer had entered my body on tiptoes and in disguise. Like a burglar dressed in black to blend in with the dark, the disease had merged with the onset of menopause. There was the new gynaecologist I saw five months before the crash, who cheerfully dismissed my concerns and sent me home without a blood test. 'You're a healthy woman, Mrs Yanikoski,' she said. Finally, there was the mind-bending nature of serious illness – something I'd never experienced before – making me feel vulnerable and intimidated, warping my judgement. I seemed to be moving in slow motion, with a heavy head and painful legs.

Long after I had ceased feeling guilty about my father's death, I still felt defined by it. Randy's diagnosis – coming at a time when I felt that I was finally making something of myself, becoming a writer – had also felt deeply personal. Though I had been a loving mother to both my children, and was always at home, writing biographies in an attic room around their schedules, I felt responsible for Randy's autism.

I had lost my father, I lived in fear of losing my husband – imagining the worst every time Chuck's commuter train was late – and I was now losing my son.

Soon after Randy's diagnosis, at about age three, I had begun suffering from panic attacks. I wondered if I had jinxed Randy by naming him after my father, whom Randy and I both resembled. But as Randy matured, I began to make sense of his autism. There was Chuck's detachment – a maddening quality that took me years to understand. How could a man who so obviously loved his wife and children be so untouchable at times, so remote? He was incapable of worrying about Randy's diagnosis or future. ('All I care about is that my children are happy, and that they are good,' said this brilliant and literate man, leaving me to deal with Randy's treatment and education. And yet he supported and appreciated my decisions.) As we drove home from the Dana-Farber in 2006 with my devastating prognosis running like a looping tape through our minds, Chuck – a man who would have done anything for me, and was now trying to alleviate my chronic worry about money, and offer some relief – began talking about our finances. Now that we knew I was not going to live into ripe old age, we wouldn't have to be quite as careful, he reflected, until I cut him off with my tears. He moved serenely through life, largely untouched by family quarrels and dramas, rarely cracking with emotion.

I began seeing the odd traits in my own family differently. There was my beloved and sweet-tempered maternal grandmother, Geema, with her hard blink and constant throat-clearing – traits so inseparable from her that when I asked my mother and uncle about it they couldn't remember that their own mother compulsively blinked and cleared her throat. They could, however, recall the odd 'nervous' twitches of Geema's brother and nephew, which they imitated with glee.

Both Chuck's family and mine claimed their share of talkers – people who talk without any social awareness. There was the interminable gabbler who fell asleep for a full half-hour on the phone while her even more loquacious sister talked on, oblivious. There was the honeymoon story about Geema's parents, married after a five-year engagement during which they had communicated only by letter while my great-grandfather, a Methodist minister, finished his education in Pennsylvania. The newly-weds were at the Portland train station, my great-grandfather so absorbed in his talk with the brother who had driven the couple to the station that he failed to notice that his stunning bride, who had exquisite features, fair Irish skin and long black hair, had been left behind on the platform. The train was beginning to pull away when he noticed and snatched her up.

And what of Randy's mother? A healthy and apparently normal little girl, I had been transformed, at age eight, into a spectacle of nervous tics and blinks. For a year after the fire, my arms and shoulders jerked involuntarily, as though someone was pulling the strings. I couldn't step on sidewalk cracks but obsessively counted them while I zigzagged my way in front of the apartment building in Portland, Oregon, the same complex where my Davis grandparents lived and where we had lived before moving with Daddy to Texas and Alabama, where he attended flight school. I developed a reading problem in which I had to reread each sentence compulsively before I could proceed to the next. I sleepwalked. I became claustrophobic.

Until recently, I attributed my own psychological problems and anxieties to childhood trauma, which didn't end, or even begin, with the house fire. But what falls away after that nightmarish year of 1961–62, after Randy's diagnosis, after the collapse of the Twin Towers on 9/11 – a mythic re-enactment of my burning house – is a portrait of a 59-year-old woman who still, during times of stress, compulsively rereads sentences. Though I essentially lost my nervous tics in childhood, I realized that I repeat some of my own sentences two or more times during a short conversation, and talk to myself out loud, as Grams did. 'I look in the mirror / Through the eyes of the child that was me,' sings Judy Collins in 'Secret Gardens', the old song that always reminds me of my Oregon childhood. I see myself and I see my son – though Randy is incapable of passing for normal. I review Chuck's family and mine, and see a continuum. It seems that we're all part of the great undiagnosed in which a fully autistic being eventually emerged.

'Mummy drives the back roads, Papa drives the highway,' notes our increasingly observant companion. But he does not divine his mother's raw fear, which makes her feel as though she's been peeled. He doesn't see that her eyes are closed when Papa takes the highway because we don't have time to take the back way.

Though Randy is happy in his small life – a patchwork plan of volunteer jobs, classes for the disabled, home chores and a dollop of paid employment (five hours a week on a good week), all recorded in a Daily Planner he hands me each evening to fill out ('You will write my Schedule, Mom) – he worries. His overriding preoccupation, very much in line with my own, is his future. Listen to his nightly recitations of *fam-i-ly his-to-ry* – delivered in a sing-song in his bedroom – and you will hear someone calculating. (He is occasionally more direct. 'Mom, live in Harvard with you and Papa for a *long* time,' he'll say, drawing out the 'o'.) He is always looking forward, toward the next birthday, the coming event – so much so that I spent all of last year trying to remember whether I was fifty-seven or fifty-eight. Though unremittingly cheerful – he laughs, sings and begins and ends every day in a good mood – he is humourless on the subject of his own adult status. 'Have you been a good little boy this year?' asked the intrusively jolly Santa at a Christmas party last year. 'Young adult man!' Randy corrected, and rushed past him.

His ever-sunny, gentle nature can obscure his anxiety about his own health and safety. 'Don't want to break a bone, don't want to go to the hospital,' he'll say before riding his bike. When I warn him about his excess weight and the dangers of overeating: 'Me – I don't want to have to go to the hospital, nobody's dying,' he'll say, breaking my heart. And yet such comments probably owe more to my frequent admonitions than to his memories of my hospitalization and illness. For all the progress he has made in twenty-six years, he still must be reminded to look both ways when he crosses a street. Last year he was almost hit by a van as I watched – a scene that played out frequently during his childhood.

Life with Randy is life under kindly surveillance by someone who is not only new to our shores, but to our planet. He is part of the family and yet an alien among us, someone still awkwardly navigating the language and culture. Take him to a Woody Allen movie, and he'll follow our lead, but with a fake laugh. Take him to *Toy Story 3* and he laughs with genuine glee. From his perch at the kitchen counter – his preferred seating, at a remove from the gathering at the round antique oak table – he keeps up a running commentary. Mention my mother, for instance: 'Granny, that's my grandmother, was Geema's daughter, Papa Lister's daughter, married to Grandpa Randy . . .'

Mention Chuck's and my wedding: 'Geema was there, Grams was there, after Grandpa Randy died, burned in a fire, before Cousin Jenny died in a car crash,' says Randy – a macabre rush in which decades are collapsed. And yet he is more than an amanuensis and sponge: he has some decided opinions of his own. He is, for instance, quick to offer that, in his family, his mother and sister swear; he and his father do not. Say something crude and the condemnation from the peanut gallery is swift and loud: 'That's disgusting, that's gross, that's nasty. No naughty words, only good words, like goodness, golly, gracious' – a Randy rant that once drove two robust Red Sox fans from their expensive seats at Fenway Park.

In Randy-speak, things often seem more poetic and funny: the tree swing Chuck made for him became a 'swing tree'. Asked how he was holding up on a humid, mosquito-infested summer day, he replied, 'Medium sweaty.'

He's the ibid., the op. cit., the heckler and Greek chorus of our lives. He's the echo chamber. 'Randy, are you ready to do the dishes?' 'Are you ready to do the dishes, Mom I'm ready to wash the dishes, Mom,' he'll say, moving toward me with his head inclined, bird-like, his right arm clamped to his chest as he repeatedly gives me the thumbs-up sign and nods his head, his eyes opened unnaturally wide in an exaggerated expression until I answer him. At which point he'll repeat himself until I tell him to stop or leave the room. At social gatherings he darts in and out, alighting on the couch to ask for 'information' or offer an irrelevant comment before zooming off like a hummingbird to his hovering point. ('Well, he didn't stay very long, did he!' says ninety-year-old Grams with a laugh in an old video I took in Oregon when the kids were little.)

He's our dishwasher, vacuumer, salad maker, firewood stacker and assistant leaf raker and snow shoveller. He's the cart pusher and unpacker on our weekly trips to the grocery store – duties duly recorded in his Daily Planner. When plans are revised he rarely protests, though he occasionally asserts his independence. 'You don't want to go with me, huh?' I said the other day when he refused an invitation to join me on some errands. 'I'm staying here,' said Randy. 'Too bad, that's sad,' he added.

Life with this funny, young adult man who listens to Christmas carols in June and is incapable of an unkind act is all we know. And life with us – first in the old house we left on June 26, 1996, a Wednesday, then in the red colonial warmed by lamplight – is all he has ever known. To be sure, it is not ideal: the burden of managing job coaches, finding volunteer work, absorbing rejections and filling Randy's Daily Planner is wearing and ultimately unsustainable. I once found myself writing a letter of resignation on Randy's behalf in response to some long-standing hostility toward him in our doctor's office, his one paid job. Though the story had a happy ending – the doctor called an emergency staff meeting and promised to fire the person responsible for discriminating against Randy if she didn't clean up her act (she did) – it is typical of the unwelcoming climate Randy works in – even as a volunteer with a coach. There is always some fresh wound, a new battle to fight. And there isn't enough work.

Even vacuum manufacturers seem to conspire against us. When I finally replaced our old upright with an expensive canister model, it came with a warning about disabled persons vacuuming without supervision. (Though Randy learned to use the new machine in a general way, he can't remember to check the warning light measuring the air flow, or heed my weekly reminders about not vacuuming up pine needles and other sharp objects that can block the hose and cause a fire.) Yet his cobbled-together life is the best one available to him now. And we love him. Do we give him up to an overwhelmed and underfunded system with an increasingly long waiting list, to an unaccepting world – and if so, when?

Since our tearful discussion with a social worker six years ago, when I was in the midst of chemo and we thought it best to ask the state for a future residential placement for Randy, we have been unable to proceed. First came Randy's trembling reaction when I introduced the idea of his living with 'friends'. Then Allie, having spent a depressing year after college working in a group home for disabled adults, insisted that she wanted Randy to live with her some day. Other relatives also stepped forward – and yet every unselfish offer seems unsustainable. Is this fair to Allie? What will her own family needs be when she marries and has children? Where will she live, and what will the services and funding be in that state? What if Allie becomes ill or dies before Randy does? (I am haunted by the memory of a cousin of Chuck's with Down's syndrome, who, after fifty-something years with her mother, who lived well into her nineties, was abruptly torn from the only home she had ever known and placed in a group home. She died soon after.)

In Massachusetts, the Department of Developmental Services currently serves only those with an IQ of seventy or below – 41 per cent of those with autism spectrum disorder. Only 10 per cent are currently getting housing. Two years ago – before the state's human services were slashed again – I was told by the DDS that because Randy functions better than many adults with autism, he would be funded (once there's a space on the waiting list, a list that grows longer as Chuck and I fail to ask for residential services for Randy) in either a semi-independent residential model, or placed in a 'shared living' home. We know Randy belongs in a family, but can strangers love him? And how do we trust them? Who will make sure Randy doesn't set fire to the place when he vacuums in a semi-supervised setting? Who will protect him from the stranger at the door?

As we keep Randy home, we may be risking his future. 'Get all the entitlements you can,' a long-time provider told us.

And how do I prepare him for my death?

I worry constantly about keeping him home too long. I do not want Randy to watch me go through chemo again – treatment bound to be more brutal the next time because 'the body remembers', Dr Niemierko told me. I never again, while in pain, want to hear myself screaming at Randy for perseverating. I cannot allow Randy to watch me die.

It tortures me to think that I won't be here to watch over him, to help him grieve.

As my remission enters year five, it is filled with uncertainty. I get a thorough check-up every six months. Two years ago, Chuck had a heart attack. Though he suffered some permanent damage, he rebounded quickly, making light of it with a line from *Casablanca*, my favourite movie. 'My heart', he joked in an email to friends, 'turns out to be my least vulnerable spot.' And yet my own heart – which is filled with Randy – is my most vulnerable spot.

'Go to the puppet show – *this* month,' Randy prods me.

'Yes, we'll go this month; I don't know what day yet,' I say. ■

CONTRIBUTORS

Chris Adrian is the author of three novels, including *The Children's Hospital*, and the story collection *A Better Angel*. He received an MD from Eastern Virginia Medical School and completed a paediatric residency and a paediatric haematology/oncology fellowship at University of California, San Francisco.

Ike Anya is a public health physician. He co-edited the *Weaverbird Collection*, an anthology of new Nigerian writing, and is co-author of nigeriahealthwatch.com.

Angela Carter (1940–92) was the author of *Shadow Dance*, *The Magic Toyshop*, *The Bloody Chamber* and *Wise Children*, among numerous other works. Her poetry collections include *Five Quiet Shouters* and *Unicorn*.

Linda H. Davis is the author of *Onward and Upward: A Biography of Katharine S. White*, *Badge of Courage: The Life of Stephen Crane* and *Charles Addams: A Cartoonist's Life*.

Brad Feuerhelm is the director of ORDINARY-LIGHT photography (ordinary-light.com), a platform for the sale of vintage and contemporary photography from around the world.

Celia Hawkesworth's recent translations include Dubravka Ugresic's *Lend Me Your Character* and Ivo Zanic's *Flag on the Mountain*.

Terrence Holt is the author of *In the Valley of the Kings*, a story collection. He teaches and practises medicine at the University of North Carolina.

M.J. Hyland is the author of three novels, including *Carry Me Down*, which was shortlisted for the Man Booker Prize. She is a lecturer in Creative Writing at the University of Manchester and co-founder of the Hyland & Byrne Editing firm. Her most recent novel is *This is How*.

Gish Jen's works include four novels, *Typical American*, *Mona in the Promised Land*, *The Love Wife* and *World and Town*, and the story collection *Who's Irish?*.

A.L. Kennedy is most recently the author of *The Blue Book*, a novel. She writes short stories, essays, screenplays and radio plays and performs stand-up comedy. She was one of *Granta*'s Best Young British Novelists in 1993 and 2003.

James Lasdun is the author, most recently, of *It's Beginning to Hurt*, a story collection. He has written three poetry books. His new collection, *Water Sessions*, is published this autumn.

Ben Lerner is the author of three books of poetry. His debut novel, *Leaving the Atocha Station*, is published in the UK by Granta Books.

Semezdin Mehmedinović is the author of *Sarajevo Blues*, *Nine Alexandrias* and *Soviet Computer*, a diary of his migration from Sarajevo to Prague and eventually Washington, DC.

Alice Munro is the author of *Dear Life: Stories*, forthcoming this autumn. Her recent collections include *The View from Castle Rock* and *Too Much Happiness*. In 2009, she was awarded the Man Booker International Prize.

Suzanne Rivecca is the author of the story collection *Death Is Not an Option*. She is the recipient of a Pushcart Prize and has twice appeared in *Best New American Voices*.

Ornan Rotem is a founder of Sylph Editions, a specialist publisher and design studio.

Kay Ryan was the sixteenth United States Poet Laureate between 2008 and 2010. She has published seven volumes of poetry and, most recently, *The Best of It: New and Selected Poems*, which won the Pulitzer Prize in 2011.

Rachel Shihor is the author of *The Vast Kingdom*, *The Tel Avivians* and *Days Bygone*. 'The Former Mayor's Ancient Daughter' is from the sequence 'Stalin is Dead', forthcoming in *Ellipsis 2*.

Rose Tremain's novels include *Music and Silence*, *Restoration*, *The Road Home* and *Trespass*. 'The Cutting' is an extract from the forthcoming novel *Merivel*, published by Chatto & Windus.